IRAQ

MIDDLE EAST
REGION IN TRANSITION
IRAQ

EDITED BY LAURA ETHEREDGE, ASSOCIATE EDITOR, MIDDLE EAST GEOGRAPHY

Britannica Educational Publishing
IN ASSOCIATION WITH
ROSEN
EDUCATIONAL SERVICES

Published in 2011 by Britannica Educational Publishing
(a trademark of Encyclopædia Britannica, Inc.)
in association with Rosen Educational Services, LLC
29 East 21st Street, New York, NY 10010.

Distributed exclusively by Rosen Educational Services.
For a listing of additional Britannica Educational Publishing titles, call toll free (800) 237-9932.

First Edition

Library of Congress Cataloging-in-Publication Data

Iraq / edited by Laura S. Etheredge.
p. cm.—(Middle East: region in transition)
"In association with Britannica Educational Publishing, Rosen Educational Services."
Includes bibliographical references and index.
ISBN 978-1-61530-304-5 (library binding)
1. Iraq. 2. Iraq—History. I. Etheredge, Laura.
DS70.62.I73 2011
956.7—dc22

2010016104

Manufactured in the United States of America

On the cover: Aside from the war-heavy headlines, Iraq pulsates with vibrant culture, people, and history (clockwise from top left): a copper craftsman in Baghdad, Muslim Shīʿites observing Āshūrā in Karbalāʾ, the modern Baghdad Palace, and the ancient city of Nineveh (opposite modern Mosul, Iraq). *(clockwise from top left) Akram Saleh/Getty Images, Mohammed Sawaf/AFP/Getty Images, Shutterstock.com, Jane Sweeney/Lonely Planet Images/ Getty Images*

On pages 1, 14, 32, 50, 62, 71, 182, 184, 187: Some Iraqi desert and mountain dwellers still depend on animals such as camels for transportation. *Francoise De Mulder/Roger Viollet/Getty Images*

CONTENTS

50

58

67

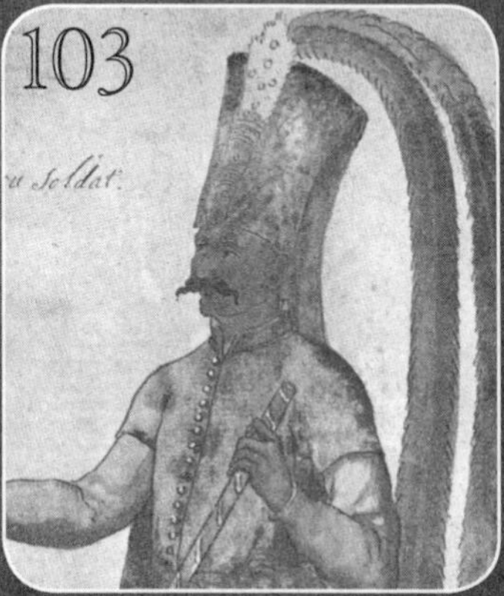
103

112

130

154

162

176

INTRODUCTION

It may seem peculiar to associate the Arabic term Al-Jazīrah ("the Island") with the nearly landlocked country of Iraq. Yet the term, which actually denotes one of Iraq's major regions, in many ways represents the country as well for the exceptional place it has occupied in history. Treasured for its fertility—it makes up much of what is known as the Fertile Crescent—Iraq has been the seat of empires and the object of desire for numerous conquerors over the centuries. This volume journeys past today's turbulent headlines to explore the history, culture, and people of a unique region that is both captivating and complex.

The topography of Iraq has largely shaped its settlement patterns and the industries that sustain the country. Perhaps among the most storied features of Iraq's landscape are the Tigris and Euphrates Rivers, whose waters nourished some of the world's earliest civilizations and remain crucial to sustaining neighbouring villages and cities and local wildlife and vegetation, as well as supporting the country's agricultural productivity. Some one-third of the country is covered by alluvial plains, which are characterized by low elevation marked by marshlands and flooding. North of the alluvial plains, the Tigris and Euphrates bound the area known as the Al-Jazīrah plateau. Like the deserts in western and southern Iraq, the plateau is largely hot and arid, but it contains some fertile soil.

The diversity of the various peoples who have settled in each of Iraq's four major regions reflects the sundry influences of past invaders and immigrants. The Arab conquests of the 7th century marked the Arabization of central and southern Iraq, and of the approximately 30

Iraq's diverse population reflects the historical influences of invaders and immigrants. AFP/Getty Images

million people in Iraq today, about two-thirds are Arabs and more than three-fourths of the population speaks one of several Arabic dialects. Another one-fourth of the population consists of Kurds, and the remainder is made up of smaller groups of Turks, Turkmen, the Lur, and Armenians.

The dominance of the Arab majority and its influence on Iraqi governance is often contrasted with the plight of the Kurdish minority. Like a significant proportion of Arab Iraqis (and like the ruling elite of much of the 20th century), Kurds are mostly Sunni Muslims. They are culturally and linguistically distinct, however, and as such, they have long struggled against Arabs for autonomy. Unable to transcend factional differences, however, Kurds have repeatedly failed to achieve statehood and have suffered intense violence against them, especially at the hands of the Baʿth regime.

Although the Iraqi population is predominantly Shīʿite, it also has a large proportion of Sunnis, thus representing both major sects of Islam more equally than any other country. Still, divisions along religious lines continue to threaten unity. Large cities like Baghdad attract diverse residents, but elsewhere in the country, settlement is generally along traditional lines: Sunni Arabs prevail in central Iraq, Kurds are concentrated in the northeast, and Shīʿites dominate the southern areas. A small number of Christians continue to reside in Iraq, but the once sizeable community of Jews has all but disappeared.

With more than two-thirds of Iraq's population settled in one of its urban centres, the country's rural communities have dwindled. Revenues from oil production have accounted for much of the shift away from agriculture toward industrialization and manufacturing. Oil is Iraq's most valuable export, and the fate of the

Iraqi economy is closely tied to its capacity to produce and distribute oil. Although Iraq at one point had the third largest economy in the Middle East, its involvement in various international conflicts produced severe economic setbacks. The devastation to oil production and distribution facilities during the Iran-Iraq War in the 1980s was compounded by the United Nations embargo on Iraq following the Iraqi invasion of Kuwait. Only after the implementation of the oil-for-food program, which allowed Iraq to sell a certain amount of oil so that it could obtain basic necessities, was the Iraqi economy able to recover to some extent.

Iraq's agricultural, manufacturing, and service sectors, as well as its trade and infrastructure, have likewise been affected by struggles with other countries. Despite widespread damage, however, Iraq remains a country still rich in many agricultural and mineral resources.

Political instability pervaded Iraq in the first half of the 20th century, first under the monarchy and then in the years following its overthrow. The socialist Baʿth Party, which came to power in 1968, brought a measure of stability, although it did not adhere to Iraq's provisional constitution. Ṣaddām Ḥussein, who ruled from 1979 until 2003, effectively turned Iraq into a dictatorship and single-party state: political parties opposing the Baʿth regime were eventually outlawed. With the toppling of the Baʿth Party at the start of the Iraq War in 2003, the legacy of unchecked power was finally abandoned. The United States and its allies subsequently helped oversee the restructuring of the Iraqi government, and a permanent constitution was approved in October 2005. The new constitution established a parliamentary democracy, with a president, a prime minister, and an independent judiciary.

Although the country remains grounded in traditional Arab and Islamic cultural values, it has also welcomed more secular trends in dress, entertainment, and women's rights, especially in its urban areas. In contrast to the elevation of ancient and traditional styles espoused by the Baʿth regime, the arts in Iraq today embrace Western styles of dance and theatre even as customary forms of Middle Eastern expression continue to be exhibited.

Evidence of Iraq's lengthy history is still visible at the country's archaeological sites, museums, and holy cities and provides insight into the country's bygone eras. Although civilization flourished in the Fertile Crescent for centuries prior to the advent of Islam, it bore little resemblance—culturally, ethnically, or socially—to current-day Iraq. The story here picks up around 600 CE, when the ethnic diversity, multiculturalism, and religious pluralism of the region at the time were challenged by new political and religious forces. In the centuries that followed, Iraq was characterized by constant transformation and reinvention.

The Persian Sāsānian empire that had overseen the stability of the region into the early 7th century finally fell to Arab Muslim conquerors in 651. Iraq subsequently became a province under the Muslim caliphate, and ʿAlī, the fourth caliph, made Iraq his centre until the Umayyad dynasty captured power and moved the seat of the caliphate to Damascus. The wealthiest part of the empire, Iraq, now subordinated, became a seat of unrest. Opposition to the Umayyads grew, and after the ʿAbbāsids succeeded in overthrowing the Umayyads in 750 the caliphate was returned to Iraq with its capital at Baghdad. Notwithstanding periods of instability, the ʿAbbāsid caliphate supervised advances in science and philosophy that travelled far beyond Baghdad and secured Iraq's place as a hub of cultural and intellectual activity.

After the decline of the ʿAbbāsids and the period of chaos that followed, an initial measure of stability was achieved when the Būyids—who allowed the ʿAbbāsid caliph to remain as a captive figurehead—assumed control of Iraq. With the subsequent descent into political turbulence, however, the region became vulnerable for capture by the Turkish Seljuqs, led by Toghrıl Beg, in 1055. In the 12th century, ʿAbbāsids rallied against the Seljuqs and confronted them militarily, and under the caliph al-Nāṣir the ʿAbbāsids were able to shake off Seljuq domination and revive independent caliphal authority. Not long after al-Nāṣir's death in 1225, Mongol invaders entered the area, and by 1258 Baghdad had fallen to them.

The destruction wrought in Iraq by the Mongols was exacerbated by the tumultuous rule of the Mongols' Timurid and Turkmen successors. Even as arts reached new heights in the 15th century, by the decline of the Turkmen Kara Koyunlu and Ak Koyunlu tribal federations, Iraq had experienced one of the darkest periods in its history.

After a period under Shīʿite Ṣafavid rule, the next phase of Iraqi history witnessed the integration of Iraq into the Ottoman Empire. Iraq was thereafter oriented westward and aligned more closely with Ottoman dominions in Syria and Anatolia than with its own neighbouring Persian lands. The Sunnism of the Ottomans prevailed in Iraq, but Shīʿites retained influence and prestige.

Ottoman rule was often unsteady and did not go unchallenged: local dynasties around Iraq as well as the Ṣafavids vied for control when the central Ottoman government weakened in the 17th century, while the Iranian leader, Nādir Shah, tried to advance on Iraq in the 18th century. Still, the Ottomans revolutionized Iraq in many respects. The governorship of Midhat Paşa, for instance, oversaw the improvement of Iraq's infrastructure and educational facilities and the introduction of the Ottoman Land Law of 1858, which systematized the process of land ownership and the collection of taxes.

The interest of Great Britain in the area had been growing since the end of the 18th century, and it was the British who ultimately led to the end of Ottoman control. The British feared the increase of German influence in Iraq, and during World War I they strove to capture Baghdad, succeeding in 1917. At the end of World War I, the League of Nations granted Great Britain a mandate to govern Iraq, which it did until 1932. During this period the British established a constitutional monarchy with the emir Fayṣal I as the king of Iraq. After Iraqis voiced concern over foreign influence, Iraq was granted independence. British influence continued thereafter, however, notable especially in such issues as Iraq's role in World War II.

Troubled by continued British involvement and their exclusion from the country's politics, younger Iraqis revolted in 1958 and deposed the monarchy. The material progress Iraq made in the 1950s thanks to the increased oil revenues it earned only marginally offset the tension in the region. The 1958 revolution was followed by more unstable regimes, first under ʿAbd al-Karīm Qāsim and then under ʿAbd al-Salām ʿĀrif, who was overthrown by the army in 1968. The Baʿth Party, which had briefly taken power in 1963, reclaimed power in 1968 and would retain it, chiefly under Pres. Ṣaddām Ḥussein, until 2003.

Iraqi history under Ṣaddām Ḥussein was dominated by international conflict. The Iran-Iraq War (1980–88) resulted from the clash of the Islamic government of Iran and the secular one of Iraq. The influence upon the Shīʿites of Iraq by Shīʿite Iran—whose policy of exporting its Islamic revolution included the desire to overthrow the

Iraqi government—was of special concern. To the detriment of both countries, Iraq and Iran fought for much of the 1980s, and a formal peace agreement was not achieved until 1990. An array of Iraqi grievances against Kuwait—including territorial disputes, Kuwaiti violation of OPEC quotas, and accusations that its neighbour had stolen Iraqi oil—led to the Iraqi invasion of Kuwait in August 1990. After suffering defeat at the hands of the United States and coalition forces, Iraq withdrew from Kuwait and ended the Persian Gulf War.

The Iraq War, begun in 2003, was launched by the United States and United Kingdom based on the notion that Iraq supported terrorist groups and planned to obtain weapons of mass destruction. The Iraq War entailed the dismantling of Ṣaddām's regime and the launch of a Western initiative to implement democracy in Iraq. Indeed, Iraq was able to hold democratic elections in the years following the war's start, but the war itself continued through the first decade of the 21st century.

Although Iraq has withstood immense hardship throughout periods of its history, its cultural bequests have continued to influence the world. Inheriting a wide range of challenges from its predecessors and confronting new questions as it moves forward, today's Iraqi government must navigate unfamiliar territory as it pioneers new solutions to each.

CHAPTER 1

LAND

Iraq is the easternmost country of the Arab world, located at about the same latitude as the southern United States. It is bordered to the north by Turkey, to the east by Iran, to the west by Syria and Jordan, and to the south by Saudi Arabia and Kuwait. Iraq has 12 miles (19 kilometre) of coastline along the northern end of the Persian Gulf, giving it a tiny sliver of territorial sea. Followed by Jordan, it is thus the Middle Eastern state with the least access to the sea and offshore sovereignty.

Iraq. Encyclopædia Britannica, Inc.

RELIEF

Iraq's topography can be divided into four physiographic regions: the alluvial plains of the central and southeastern parts of the country; Al-Jazīrah (Arabic: "the Island"), an upland region in the north between the Tigris and

Fertile Crescent

The Fertile Crescent is the region in the Middle East where the civilizations of the Middle East and the Mediterranean basin began. The term was popularized by the American Orientalist James Henry Breasted.

The Fertile Crescent includes a roughly crescent-shaped area of relatively fertile land that probably had a more moderate, agriculturally productive climate in the past than today, especially in Mesopotamia and the Nile valley. Situated between the Arabian Desert to the south and the mountains of Armenia to the north, it extends from Babylonia and adjacent Susiana (the southwestern province of Persia) up the Tigris and Euphrates rivers to Assyria. From the Zagros Mountains east of Assyria, it continues westward over Syria to the Mediterranean and extends southward to southern Palestine. The Nile valley of Egypt is often included as a further extension, especially because the short interruption in Sinai is no greater than similar desert breaks that disturb its continuity in Mesopotamia and Syria. Throughout the region irrigation is necessary for the best agricultural results and, indeed, is often essential to any farming at all.

In its wider extension, the Fertile Crescent corresponds exactly to the region that plays a dominant role in the Hebrew traditions of Genesis and contains the ancient countries (Babylonia, Assyria, Egypt, Phoenicia) from which the Greeks and Romans derived civilization. This age-old belief that the earliest known culture originated in the Fertile Crescent has been confirmed by the development of radiocarbon dating since 1948. It is now known that incipient agriculture and village agglomerations there must be dated back to about 8000 BCE, if not earlier, and that the use of irrigation followed rapidly.

Euphrates rivers; deserts in the west and south; and the highlands in the northeast. Each region extends into neighbouring countries, but the alluvial plains lie largely within Iraq.

Alluvial Plains

The plains of lower Mesopotamia extend southward some 375 miles (600 km) from Balad on the Tigris and Al-Ramādī on the Euphrates to the Persian Gulf. They cover more than 51,000 square miles (132,000 square km), almost one-third of the country's area, and are characterized by low elevation, below 300 feet (100 metres), and poor natural drainage. Large areas are subject to widespread seasonal flooding, and there are extensive marshlands, some of which dry up in the summer to become salty wastelands. Near Al-Qurnah, where the Tigris and Euphrates converge to form the Shatt al-Arab, there are still some inhabited marshes. The alluvial plains contain extensive lakes. The swampy Lake Al-Ḥammār (Hawr al-Ḥammār) extends 70 miles (110 km) from Al-Baṣrah (Basra) to Sūq al-Shuyūkh; its width varies from 8 to 15 miles (13 to 25 km).

Al-Jazīrah

North of the alluvial plains, between the Tigris and the Euphrates rivers, is the arid Al-Jazīrah plateau. Its most prominent hill range is the Sinjār Mountains, whose highest peak reaches an elevation of 4,448 feet (1,356 m). The main watercourse is the Wadi Al-Tharthār, which runs southward for 130 miles (210 km) from the Sinjār Mountains to the Tharthār (Salt) Depression. Milḥat Ashqar is the largest of several salt flats (or *sabkhahs*) in the region.

The Euphrates River at Khān al-Baghdādī, on the edge of Al-Jazīrah plateau in north-central Iraq. © Nik Wheeler

Deserts

Western and southern Iraq is a vast desert region covering some 64,900 square miles (168,000 square km), almost two-fifths of the country. The western desert, an extension of the Syrian Desert, rises to elevations above 1,600 feet (490 m). The southern desert is known as Al-Ḥajarah in the western part and as Al-Dibdibah in the east. Al-Ḥajarah has a complex topography of rocky desert, wadis, ridges, and depressions. Al-Dibdibah is a more sandy region with a covering of scrub vegetation. Elevation in the southern desert averages between 300 and 1,200 feet (100 to 400 m). A height of 3,119 feet (951 m) is reached at Mount 'Unayzah ('Unāzah) at the intersection of the borders of Jordan, Iraq, and Saudi Arabia. The deep Wadi Al-Bāṭin runs 45 miles (75 km) in a northeast-southwest direction through Al-Dibdibah. It has been recognized since 1913 as the boundary between western Kuwait and Iraq.

The Northeast

The mountains, hills, and plains of northeastern Iraq occupy some 35,500 square miles (92,000 square km), about one-fifth of the country. Of this area only about one-fourth is mountainous, and the remainder is a complex transition zone between mountain and lowland. The ancient kingdom of Assyria was located in this area. North and northeast of the Assyrian plains and foothills is Kurdistan, a mountainous region that extends into Turkey and Iran.

The relief of northeastern Iraq rises from the Tigris toward the Turkish and Iranian borders in a series of rolling plateaus, river basins, and hills until the high mountain ridges of Iraqi Kurdistan, associated with the Taurus and Zagros mountains, are reached. These mountains are aligned northwest to southeast and are separated by river basins where human settlement is possible. The mountain summits have an average elevation of about 8,000 feet (2,400 m), rising to 10,000–11,000 feet (3,000–3,300 m) in places. There, along the Iran-Iraq border, is the country's highest point, Ghundah Zhur, which reaches 11,834 feet (3,607 m). The region is heavily dissected by numerous tributaries of the Tigris, notably the Great and Little Zab rivers and the Diyālā and 'Uẓaym (Adhaim) rivers. These streams weave tortuously south and southwest, cutting through ridges in a number of gorges, notably the Rū Kuchūk gorge, northeast of Barzān, and the Bēkma gorge, west of Rawāndūz town. The highest mountain ridges contain the only forestland in Iraq.

DRAINAGE

Iraq is drained by the Tigris-Euphrates river system, although less than half of the Tigris-Euphrates basin lies in the country. Both rivers rise in the Armenian highlands of Turkey, where they are fed by melting winter snow. The Tigris flows 881 miles (1,417 km) and the Euphrates 753 miles (1,212 km) through Iraq before they join near Al-Qurnah to form the Shatt al-Arab, which flows another 68 miles (109 km) into the Persian Gulf. The Tigris, all of whose tributaries are on its left (east) bank, runs close to the high Zagros Mountains, from which it receives a number of important tributaries, notably the Great Zab, the Little Zab, and the Diyālā. As a result, the Tigris can be subject to devastating floods, as evidenced by the many old channels left when the river carved out a new course. The period of maximum flow of the Tigris is from March

Diyālā River

The Diyālā River (Arabic: Nahr Diyālā) is an important tributary of the Tigris River. It rises in the Zagros Mountains of western Iran near Hamadān as the Sīrvān River and flows westward across lowlands to join the Tigris just below Baghdad. Its total length is 275 miles (443 km). The upper Diyālā drains an extensive mountain area of Iran and Iraq, and for 20 miles (32 km) it forms the frontier between the two countries. Thereafter it flows first into a rolling plateau country, forming part of the region known as Assyria and centred on the oil-field area of Khānaqīn, then through the Ḥamrīn Mountains (the southwestern boundary of Assyria) into the flat Tigris lowlands. Several dams, including the Khan Gorge, near the Iranian frontier, divert water for flood control, hydroelectric power, and the irrigation of wheat, rye, cotton, rice, and tobacco in the lower valley. Ba'qūbah, the main riparian centre, lies on the river's lower course, about 30 miles (48 km) northeast of Baghdad.

to May, when more than two-fifths of the annual total discharge may be received. The Euphrates, whose flow is roughly 50 percent greater than that of the Tigris, receives no large tributaries in Iraq.

Many dams are needed on the rivers and their tributaries to control flooding and permit irrigation. Iraq has giant irrigation projects at Bēkma, Bādūsh, and Al-Fatḥah. In the late 1970s and early '80s, Iraq completed a large-scale project that connected the Tigris and Euphrates. A canal emerges from the Tigris near Sāmarrā' and continues southwest to Lake Al-Tharthār, and another extends from the lake to the Euphrates near Al-Ḥabbāniyyah. This connection is crucial because in years of drought—aggravated by more recent upstream use of Euphrates water by Turkey and Syria—the river level is extremely low. In 1990

Syria and Iraq reached an agreement to share the water on the basis of 58 percent to Iraq and 42 percent to Syria of the total that enters Syria. Turkey, for its part, unilaterally promised to secure an annual minimum flow at its border with Syria. There is no tripartite agreement.

Following the Persian Gulf War, the Iraqi government dedicated considerable resources to digging two large canals in the south of the country, with the apparent goal of improving irrigation and agricultural drainage. There is evidence, however, that these channels were also used to drain large parts of Iraq's southern marshlands, from which rebel forces had carried out attacks against government forces. The first was reportedly designed to irrigate some 580 square miles (1,500 square km) of desert. The vast operation to create it produced a canal roughly 70 miles (115 km) long between Dhī Qār and Al-Baṣrah governorates. The second, an even grander scheme, was reportedly designed to irrigate an area some 10 times larger than the first. This canal, completed in 1992, extends from Al-Yūsufiyyah, 25 miles (40 km) south of Baghdad, to Al-Baṣrah, a total of some 350 miles (565 km).

The two projects eventually drained some nine-tenths of Iraq's southern marshes, once the largest wetlands system in the Middle East. Much of the drained area rapidly turned to arid salt flats. Following the start of the Iraq War in 2003, some parts of those projects were dismantled, but experts estimated that rehabilitation of the marshes would be impossible without extensive efforts and the expenditure of great resources.

SOILS

The desert regions have poorly developed soils of coarse texture containing many stones and unweathered rock fragments. Plant growth is limited because of aridity, and the humus content is low. In northwestern Iraq, soils vary considerably: some regions with steep slopes are badly eroded, while the river valleys and basins contain some light fertile soils. In northwest Al-Jazīrah, there is an area of potentially fertile soils similar to those found in much of the Fertile Crescent. Lowland Iraq is covered by heavy alluvial soils, with some organic content and a high proportion of clays, suitable for cultivation and for use as a building material.

Salinity, caused in part by overirrigation, is a serious problem that affects about two-thirds of the land; as a result, large areas of agricultural land have had to be abandoned. A high water table and poor drainage, coupled with high rates of evaporation, cause alkaline salts to accumulate at or near the surface in sufficient quantities to limit agricultural productivity. Reversing the effect is a difficult and lengthy process.

Heavy soil erosion in parts of Iraq, some of it induced by overgrazing and deforestation, leaves soils exposed to markedly seasonal precipitation. The Tigris-Euphrates river system has thus created a large alluvial deposit at its mouth, so that the Persian Gulf coast is much farther south than in Babylonian times.

CLIMATE

Iraq has two climatic provinces: the hot, arid lowlands, including the alluvial plains and the deserts; and the damper northeast, where the higher elevation produces cooler temperatures. In the northeast cultivation fed by precipitation is possible, but elsewhere irrigation is essential.

In the lowlands there are two seasons, summer and winter, with short transitional periods between them. Summer, which lasts from May to October, is characterized by clear skies, extremely high temperatures, and low relative humidity. No precipitation occurs between June and September. In Baghdad, July and August mean daily temperatures reach the mid-90s F (mid-30s C), and summer temperatures in the low 120s F (low 50s C) have been recorded. The diurnal temperatures range in summer is considerable.

In winter the paths of westerly atmospheric depressions crossing the Middle East shift southward, bringing rain to southern Iraq. Annual totals vary considerably from year to year, but mean annual precipitation in the lowlands ranges from about 4 to 7 inches (100 to 180 mm), nearly all of which occurs between November and April.

Winter in the lowlands lasts from December to February. Temperatures are generally mild, although extremes of hot and cold, including frosts, can occur. Winter temperatures in Baghdad range from about the mid-30s to low 60s °F (about 2 to 15 °C).

In the northeast the summer is shorter than in the lowlands, lasting from June to September, and the winter considerably longer. The summer is generally dry and hot, but average temperatures are some 5–10 °F (3–6 °C) cooler than those of lowland Iraq. Winters can be cold because of the region's high relief and the influence of northeasterly winds that bring continental air from Central Asia. In Mosul (Al-Mawṣil), January temperatures range between the mid-20s and low 60s °F (about -4 and 15 °C), with readings recorded as low as 12 °F (-11 °C).

In the foothills of the northeast, annual precipitation of 12 to 22 inches (300 to 560 mm), enough to sustain good seasonal pasture, is typical. Precipitation may exceed 40 inches (1000 mm) in the mountains, much of which falls as snow. As in the lowlands, there is little precipitation during the summer.

Shamāl

The *shamāl* is a hot and dry, dusty wind from the north or northwest in Iraq, Iran, and the Arabian Peninsula. In June and July it blows almost continuously, but usually under about 30 miles (50 km) per hour. The wind causes great dust storms, especially in July, when Baghdad may experience five or more such storms. The *shamāl* is part of a widespread flow toward a low-pressure centre over Pakistan.

A steady northerly and northwesterly summer wind, the *shamāl*, affects all of Iraq. It brings extremely dry air, so hardly any clouds form, and the land surface is thus heated intensively by the sun. Another wind, the *sharqī* (Arabic: "easterly"), blows from the south and southeast during early summer and early winter. It is often accompanied by dust storms. Dust storms occur throughout Iraq during most of the year and may rise to great height in the atmosphere. They are particularly frequent in summer, with five or six striking central Iraq in July, the peak of the season.

PLANT AND ANIMAL LIFE

Vegetation in Iraq reflects the dominant influence of drought. Some Mediterranean and alpine plant species thrive in the mountains of Kurdistan, but the open oak forests that formerly were found there have largely disappeared. Hawthorns, junipers, terebinths, and wild pears grow on the lower mountain slopes. A steppe region of open, treeless vegetation is located in the area extending north and northeast from the Ḥamrīn Mountains up to the foothills and lower slopes of the mountains of Iraqi

Kurdistan. A great variety of herbs and shrubs grow in that region. Most belong to the sage and daisy families: mugwort (*Artemisis vulgaris*), goosefoot, milkweed, thyme, and various rhizomic plants are examples. There also are many different grasses. Toward the riverine lowlands many other plants appear, including storksbill and plantain. Willows, tamarisks, poplars, licorice plants, and bullrushes grow along the banks of the lower Tigris and Euphrates rivers. The juice of the licorice plant is extracted for commercial purposes. Dozens of varieties of date palm flourish throughout southern Iraq, where the date palm dominates

Wild pigs roam in the marshland between the Tigris and Euphrates rivers in southern Iraq. © Nik Wheeler

the landscape. The lakesides and marshlands support many varieties of reeds, sedges, pimpernels, vetches, and geraniums. By contrast, vegetation in the desert regions is sparse, with tamarisk, milfoil, and various plants of the genera *Ziziphus* and *Salsola* being characteristic.

Birds are easily the most conspicuous form of wildlife. Although there are many resident species, the effect of large-scale drainage of the southern wetlands on migrants and seasonal visitors—which were once numerous—has not been fully determined. The lion and oryx have become extinct in Iraq, and the ostrich and wild ass face extinction. Wolves, foxes, jackals, hyenas, wild pigs, and wildcats are found, as well as many small animals such as martens, badgers, otters, porcupines, and muskrats. Marcia's gazelle survives in certain remote desert locations. Rivers, streams, and lakes are well stocked with a variety of fish, notably carp, various species of *Barbus*, catfish, and loach. In common with other regions of the Middle East, Iraq is a breeding ground for the unwelcome desert locust.

CHAPTER 2

People

The ancient Semitic peoples of Iraq, the Babylonians and Assyrians, and the non-Semitic Sumerians were long ago assimilated by successive waves of immigrants. The Arab conquests of the 7th century brought about the Arabization of central and southern Iraq. A mixed population of Kurds and Arabs inhabit a transition zone between those areas and Iraqi Kurdistan in the northeast. Roughly two-thirds of Iraq's people are Arabs, about one-fourth are Kurds.

In addition to the Arab and Kurdish majority groups, small communities of Turks, Turkmen, and Assyrians survive in northern Iraq. The Lur, a group speaking an Iranian language, live near the Iranian border, and a small number of Armenians are found predominantly in Baghdad and in pockets throughout the north.

About two-thirds of Iraq's population are Arab, and about one-fourth are Kurds; there are also smaller minority groups. AFP/Getty Images

ARABS

Iraq's Arab population is divided between Sunni Muslims and the more numerous Shīʿites. These groups, however, are for the most part ethnically and linguistically homogenous, and—as is common throughout the region—both value family relations strongly. Many Arabs, in fact, identify more strongly with their family or tribe (an extended, patrilineal group) than with national or confessional affiliations, a significant factor contributing to ongoing difficulties in maintaining a strong central government. This challenge is amplified by the numerical size of many extended kin groups—tribal units may number thousands or tens of thousands of members—and the consequent political and economic clout they wield. Tribal affiliation among Arab groups has continued to play an important role in Iraqi politics, and even in areas where tribalism has eroded with time (such as major urban centres), family bonds have remained close. Several generations may live in a single household (although this is more common among rural families), and family-owned-and-operated businesses are the standard. Such households tend to be patriarchal, with the eldest male leading the family.

KURDS

Although estimates of their precise numbers vary, the Kurds are reckoned to be the fourth-largest ethnic group in the Middle East, following Arabs, Turks, and Persians. There are important Kurdish minorities in Iraq, Iran, Turkey, and Syria, and Iraq's Kurds are concentrated in the relatively inaccessible mountains of Iraqi Kurdistan, which is roughly contiguous with Kurdish regions in those other countries. Kurds constitute a separate and distinctive cultural group. They are mostly Sunni Muslims who speak one of two dialects of the Kurdish language, an Indo-European language closely related to Modern Persian. They have a strong tribal structure and distinctive costume, music, and dance.

The Kurdish people were thwarted in their ambitions for statehood after World War I, and the Iraqi Kurds have since resisted inclusion in the state of Iraq. At various times the Kurds have been in undisputed control of large tracts of territory. Attempts to reach a compromise with the Kurds in their demands for autonomy, however, have ended in failure, owing partly to government pressure and partly to the inability of Kurdish factional groups to maintain a united front against successive Iraqi governments. From 1961 to 1975, aided by military support from Iran, they were intermittently in open rebellion against the Iraqi government, as they were during the Iran-Iraq War in the 1980s and again, supported largely by the United States, throughout the 1990s.

After its rise to power, the Baʿth regime of Ṣaddām Ḥussein consistently tried to extend its control into Kurdish areas through threats, coercion, violence, and, at times, the forced internal transfer of large numbers of Kurds. Intermittent Kurdish rebellions in the last quarter of the 20th century killed tens of thousands of Kurds—both combatants and noncombatants—at the hands of government forces and on various occasions forced hundreds of thousands of Kurds to flee to neighbouring Iran and Turkey. Government attacks were violent and ruthless and included the use of chemical weapons against Kurdish civilians. Such incidents took place at the village of Ḥalabjah and elsewhere in 1988.

Following a failed Kurdish uprising in the wake of the Persian Gulf War, the United States and other members of the coalition that it led against Iraq established a "safe haven" for the Kurds in an area north of latitude 36° N that was under the protection of the international community. Thereafter, the Kurds were largely autonomous until the establishment of a new Iraqi provisional government in 2003.

LANGUAGES

More than three-fourths of the people speak Arabic, the official language, which has several major dialects. These generally mutually intelligible, but significant variations do exist within the country, which makes spoken parlance between some groups (and with Arabic-speaking groups in adjacent countries) difficult. Modern Standard Arabic—the benchmark of literacy—is taught in schools, and most Arabs and many non-Arabs, even those who lack schooling, are able to understand it. Roughly one-fifth of the population speaks Kurdish, in one of its two main dialects. Kurdish is the official language in the Kurdish Autonomous Region in the north. A number of other languages are spoken by smaller ethnic groups, including Turkish, Turkmen, Azerbaijanian, and Syriac. Although Persian was once commonly spoken, it is now seldom heard. Bilingualism is fairly common, particularly among minorities who are conversant in Arabic. English is widely used in commerce.

RELIGION

Iraq is predominantly a Muslim country, in which the two major sects of Islam are represented more equally than in any other state. Largely for political reasons, however, the government has not maintained careful statistics on the relative proportion of the Sunni and Shīʿite populations.

Shīʿites

Slightly more than half (and according to some sources as many as three-fifths) of the population are Shīʿite, most of whom are Arab. Iraq's Shīʿites, like their coreligionists in Iran, follow the Ithnā ʿAsharī, or Twelver, rite.

Iraq has traditionally been the physical and spiritual centre of Shīʿism in the Islamic world. Shīʿism's two most important holy cities, Al-Najaf and Karbalāʾ, are located in southern Iraq, as is Al-Kūfah, sanctified as the site of the assassination of ʿAlī, the fourth caliph, in the 7th

Madrasahs remain important educational institutions in Iraq into modern times. Ghaith Abdul-Ahad/Getty Images

century. Sāmarrā', near Baghdad, is also of great cultural and religious significance to Shīʿites as the site of the life and disappearance of the 12th, and eponymous, imam, Muḥammad al-Mahdī al-Ḥujjah. In premodern times southern and eastern Iraq formed a cultural and religious meeting place between the Arab and Persian Shīʿite worlds, and religious scholars moved freely between the two regions. Even until relatively recent times, large numbers of notable Iranian scholars could be found studying

Karbalā'

The city of Karbalā' (also spelled Kerbela), the capital of Karbalā' *muḥāfaẓah* (governorate), is located in central Iraq. It is one of Shīʿite Islam's foremost holy cities and lies 55 miles (88 km) southwest of Baghdad, with which it is connected by rail.

The city's religious significance derives from the Battle of Karbalā' (680 CE), a one-sided contest in which al-Ḥusayn ibn 'Alī, the Shīʿite leader and grandson of the Prophet Muhammad, and his small party were massacred by a much larger force sent by the Umayyad caliph Yazīd I. Ḥusayn's tomb, located in the city, is one of the most important Shīʿite shrines and pilgrimage centres. (Sunni Wahhābī raiders destroyed it in 1801, but it was soon rebuilt.) Shīʿite Muslims consider burial in one of the city's many cemeteries a sure means of reaching paradise. The city's religious community has maintained close ties with coreligionists in Iran, and a significant portion of Karbalā''s population is of Iranian descent. Large numbers of Iranians likewise visit the city during pilgrimages to Ḥusayn's tomb.

Karbalā' still functions as a trade centre and a departure point for the pilgrimage to Mecca. The city's older section is enclosed by a wall, with the newer buildings to the south. Karbalā' has been a centre of discontent with the country's rulers. Civil discord was brutally put down there after the Persian Gulf War (1990–91). The city suffered little damage during the initial phase (2003) of the Iraq War, but it has been subject to violence since then.

or teaching in the great madrasahs (religious schools) in Al-Najaf and Karbalā'.

SUNNIS

Some two-fifths of the Iraqi population are Sunni. The Sunni community is divided mainly between Arabs and Kurds but includes other smaller groups, such as Azerbaijanis and Turkmen. Regionally, Sunni Arabs have traditionally predominated in central Iraq.

Since the inception of the Iraqi state in 1920, the ruling elites have consisted mainly—although not exclusively—of minority Sunni Arabs. Among these, Ṣaddām Ḥussein (president of Iraq from 1979 to 2003) was particularly well known for variably coopting, repressing, and persecuting the Iraqi Shīʿite population during his rule. Most Sunni Arabs follow the Ḥanafī school of jurisprudence and most Kurds the Shāfiʿī school, but this distinction has lost the meaning that it had in earlier times.

Ḥanafiyyah

In Islam the Ḥanafī school represents one of the four Sunni schools of religious law, incorporating the legal opinions of the ancient Iraqi schools of al-Kūfah and Al-Baṣrah. Ḥanafī legal thought (*madhhab*) developed from the teachings of the theologian Abū Ḥanīfah (*c.* 699–767) by such disciples as Abū Yūsuf (d. 798) and Muḥammad al-Shaybānī (749/50–805) and became the official system of Islamic legal interpretation of the ʿAbbāsids, Seljuqs, and Ottomans. Although the Ḥanafīs acknowledge the Qur'ān and Hadith (narratives concerning the Prophet's life and sayings) as primary sources of law, they are noted for the acceptance of personal opinion (*ra'y*) in the absence of precedent. The school currently predominates in Central Asia, India, Pakistan, Turkey, and the countries of the former Ottoman Empire.

Religious Minorities

Followers of other religions include Christians and even smaller groups of Yazīdīs, Mandaeans, Jews, and Bahā'īs. The nearly extinct Jewish community traces its origins to the Babylonian Exile (586–516 BCE). Jews formerly constituted a small but significant minority and were largely concentrated in or around Baghdad, but, with the rise of Zionism, anti-Jewish feelings became widespread. This tension eventually led to the massive Farhūd pogrom of June 1941. With the establishment of Israel in 1948, most Jews emigrated there or elsewhere. The Christian communities are chiefly descendants of the ancient population that was not converted to Islam in the 7th century. They are subdivided among various sects, including Nestorians (Assyrians), Chaldeans—who broke with the Nestorians in the 16th century and are now affiliated with the Roman Catholic church—Monophysite Jacobites, and members of the Eastern Orthodox churches.

SETTLEMENT PATTERNS

Iraq has a relatively low population density overall. In the fertile lowlands and the cities, however, densities are nearly four times the national average.

Rural Settlement

The distribution of towns and villages in Iraq follows basic patterns established thousands of years ago. Although the proportion of rural dwellers has fallen to less than one-fourth of the total population, the actual number remains comparatively high. Today several thousand villages and hamlets are scattered unevenly throughout the two-thirds

Rural dwellers, who account for more than one-third of the Iraqi population, live in one of the many villages and hamlets strewn across the country. Oleg Nikishin/Getty Images

of Iraq that is permanently settled. The greatest concentration of villages is in the valleys and lowlands around the Tigris and Euphrates. Most have between 100 and 2,000 houses, traditionally clustered tightly for defensive purposes. Their populations are engaged almost exclusively in agriculture, although essential services are located in the larger villages.

Villages in the foothills and mountains of the largely Kurdish northeast tend to be smaller and more isolated than those of lowland Iraq, which befits a lifestyle that is based on animal husbandry and only rarely on agriculture. The arid and semiarid areas in the west and south have sparse populations. The arid regions, along with the extensive Al-Jazīrah region northwest of Baghdad, were traditionally inhabited by nomadic Bedouin tribes, but few of these people remain in Iraq. Another lifestyle under threat is that of the Shīʿite marsh dwellers (Madan) of southern Iraq. They traditionally have lived in reed dwellings built on brushwood foundations or sandspits, but the damage done to the marshes in the 1990s has largely undermined their way of living. Rice, fish, and edible rushes have been staples, supplemented by products of the water buffalo.

Urban Settlement

More than two-thirds of Iraq's population are urban dwellers, and almost two-fifths of those are concentrated in the five largest cities: Baghdad, Al-Baṣrah, Mosul, Arbīl, and Al-Sulaymāniyyah. The country's one major conurbation is Baghdad, a metropolis of more than 5,000,000, but most cities have populations between 50,000 and 500,000. There are also a considerable number of small towns, many of which are market centres, provincial capitals, or

With a population of more than 5 million people, Baghdad is by far the country's largest conurbation. Sabah Arar/AFP/Getty Images

the headquarters of smaller local government districts. Attempts to stimulate the growth of selected small towns have had only modest success, and government efforts to stem the tide of people departing rural areas, through agricultural reform and other measures, have largely failed.

Baghdad

For a variety of reasons, rural migrants have been particularly drawn to Baghdad, the country's political, economic, and communications hub. First, to minimize the danger of riots in the capital city, the Baʿth regime—in addition to a variety of security measures—made special efforts to maintain a minimal level of public services, even in the poorest neighbourhoods. This was especially important after the United Nations (UN) imposed an extended embargo on Iraqi trade in response to Iraq's invasion of Kuwait in 1990, when food rationing became more necessary than ever before. Distributing rations has been more efficient in the capital area. Second, chances for employment typically have been better in Baghdad than in other cities. This was true as early as the 1930s, when migrants began to move to the city. Since that time, Shīʿite Arabs from the south have been the largest migrant group in the city, a trend that was enhanced during the Iran-Iraq War as many refugees fled the southern war zones. Efforts to limit this influx, and even reverse it, have met with only limited success; and by the beginning of the 21st century, Shīʿite Arabs represented a majority in the capital. The poor Shīʿite-Arab Al-Thawrah ("Revolution") quarter—known between 1982 and 2003 as Ṣaddām's City—alone houses some two million people. According to official statistics in the early 1990s, more than one-fifth of the country's population lived in the governorate of Baghdad, almost all of them in the city itself. In reality, the figures were probably closer to one-third.

It is no coincidence that Baghdad's celebrated predecessors, Babylon and the Sāsānian capital, Ctesiphon, were located in the same general region. Baghdad, itself a city of legend, is located at the heart of what has long been a rich agricultural region, and the modern city is the undisputed commercial, manufacturing, and service capital of Iraq. Its growth, however, has necessitated costly projects, including elaborate flood-prevention schemes completed largely in the 1950s, the rehousing of hundreds of thousands of inhabitants of squalid shantytowns (*ṣarīfahs*) in the 1960s (and, on a much smaller scale, in 1979–80), and the construction of major domestic water and sewerage projects. The city was damaged during both the Persian Gulf War and the Iraq War and required major reconstruction of all parts of the infrastructure.

Regional Centres

Al-Baṣrah, on the west bank of the Shatt al-Arab and formerly Iraq's main port, is the centre of its southern petroleum sector and the hub of the country's date cultivation. One of the great cities of Islamic history and heritage, it was badly damaged and largely depopulated during the Iran-Iraq War. Although partially reconstructed following that conflict, it again suffered during the Persian Gulf War and subsequent fighting between Shīʿite rebels and government forces. Much of the city's infrastructure (sewerage and potable water and health care facilities) remained in a state of disarray, with dire results for public health. Al-Baṣrah's function as a port has been taken over by Umm Qaṣr, a small shallow-water port on the gulf.

Iraq's third city, now its second largest in terms of population, is Mosul, which is situated on the Tigris near the ruins of the ancient Assyrian capital of Nineveh. Mosul is the centre for the upper Tigris basin, specializing in processing and marketing agricultural and animal products.

It has grown rapidly, partly as a result of the influx of Kurdish refugees fleeing government repression in Iraqi Kurdistan. By the end of the 1990s, Mosul too had suffered from government neglect, and, relative to Baghdad, its infrastructure and health care facilities were in poor condition. As a result, the level of child malnutrition found in Mosul, though to a lesser extent than in Al-Baṣrah, is far higher than is experienced in the capital.

Al-Baṣrah

Al-Baṣrah is a city located in southeastern Iraq. It is situated on the western bank of the Shatt al-Arab (the waterway formed by the union of the Tigris and Euphrates rivers) at its exit from Lake Al-Ḥammār, 70 miles (110 km) by water above Al-Fāw (Fao) on the Persian Gulf. The adjacent terrain is low-lying and deeply intersected by creeks and small watercourses.

Al-Baṣrah was founded as a military encampment by the second caliph, ʿUmar I, in 638 CE about 8 miles (13 km) from the modern town of Al-Zubayr, Iraq. Its proximity to the Persian Gulf and easy access to both the Tigris and Euphrates rivers and the eastern frontiers encouraged its growth into a real city, in spite of the harsh climate and the difficulty of supplying the camp with drinking water. The first architecturally significant mosque in Islam was constructed there in 665.

Basran troops fought the Sāsānian Persians at Nahāvand (642) and conquered the western provinces of Iran (650), while the town itself was the site of the Battle of the Camel (656), an encounter between ʿĀʾishah, the Prophet Muhammad's widow, and ʿAlī, Muhammad's son-in-law and fourth caliph. In the years during and after ʿAlī's caliphate (656–661), Al-Baṣrah was a focus of the political strife that arose between the competing religious factions in Islam. This political friction was intensified by a volatile social situation. The Arab army constituted an aristocracy in Al-Baṣrah, whereas the local and various migrant peoples who had settled there (Indians, Persians, Africans, Malays) were merely *mawālī*, or clients attached to Arab tribes. Basran history from the late 7th century is thus one of unrest and insurrection. The city was seized briefly by the forces of a claimant of the caliphate, ʿAbd Allāh ibn al-Zubayr (died 692), then became the centre of Ibn al-Ashʿath's revolt in 701 and al-Muhallab's revolt in 719–720.

Conditions did not improve under the ʿAbbāsids, who took over the caliphate in 750. The uprisings continued: the Zoṭṭ, an Indian people, rose up in 820–835; the Zanj, African blacks brought into Mesopotamia for agricultural slave labour, rebelled about 869–883. The Qarmatians, an extremist Muslim sect, invaded and devastated Al-Baṣrah in 923, and thereafter the city declined, overshadowed by the prominence of the ʿAbbāsid capital, Baghdad. By the 14th century, neglect and the Mongol invasions left little of the original Al-Baṣrah standing, and by the turn of the 16th century it was relocated at the site of ancient Al-Ubullah, a few miles upstream.

Al-Baṣrah had been, however, a brilliant cultural centre in its own right throughout the 8th and into the 9th century. It was the home of noted Arab grammarians, poets, prose writers, and literary and religious scholars. Islamic mysticism was first introduced in Al-Baṣrah by al-Ḥasan al-Baṣrī, and the theological school of the Muʿtazilah developed there. Al-Baṣrah is perhaps best known to Westerners as the city from which Sinbad set out in *The Thousand and One Nights.*

Al-Baṣrah was taken by the Turks in 1668. In the 17th and 18th centuries, English, Dutch, and Portuguese traders became established there, and Al-Baṣrah developed considerably during the 19th century as a transshipment point for river traffic to Baghdad. In 1914 the construction of a modern harbour was begun at Al-Baṣrah, which previously had had no wharves. During World War I the British occupied Al-Baṣrah and used it as the port whereby communications were maintained between Mesopotamia and India. Under the ensuing British mandate, many improvements were effected in the city, and both the town and port grew in importance. In 1930 the port installations were transferred from British to Iraqi ownership. During World War II the Allies sent supplies to their Soviet allies through Al-Baṣrah.

The growth of Iraq's petroleum industry in the postwar decades turned Al-Baṣrah into a major petroleum refining and exporting centre. Before the Iran-Iraq War (1980–88), petroleum was pumped from Al-Baṣrah to the town of Al-Fāw, on the Persian Gulf, and loaded on tankers for export. Al-Baṣrah's refinery was much damaged in the opening months of the Iran-Iraq War, however, and many of the city's buildings were destroyed by artillery bombardments as the Iranians advanced to within less than 6 miles (10 km) of it in 1987. The city again suffered extensive damage in 1991 during the Persian Gulf War and in subsequent fighting between rebel factions and government troops.

Al-Baṣrah was also affected by the Iraq War, which commenced in March 2003. The city's garrison was deemed too great a threat to the U.S.-led coalition's supply lines, and, shortly after the onset of the war, British troops engaged in a methodical siege operation against Iraqi army and paramilitary forces in and around the city. After two weeks of fighting, Al-Baṣrah fell. British armed forces occupied and governed the region until December 2007, when security responsibilities were returned to the Iraqi government.

The modern city of Al-Baṣrah is an agglomeration of three small towns, Al-Baṣrah, Al-'Ashār, and Al-Ma'qil, and several small villages. Around these settlements are extensive palm groves intersected by drainage canals and minor inlets to a width of about 3 miles (5 km) from the Shatt al-Arab. Al-Baṣrah is situated in an area that is very productive agriculturally in spite of its large swampy tracts, many of which were drained in the early 1990s. Crops grown include dates, corn (maize), rice, and millet.

DEMOGRAPHIC TRENDS

Iraq is one of the most populous countries of the Middle East. Yet demographic information since 1980 has been difficult to obtain and interpret, and outside observers often have been forced to use estimates. From 1990 on a UN embargo on Iraq, which made travel to and from the country difficult, contributed considerably to the lack of information, but most important was the rule of more than 30 years by the Ba'thist regime, which was intent on controlling the flow of information about the country. The former Iraqi government sought to downplay unflattering demographic shifts in its Kurdish and Shī'ite communities while highlighting the effects of the UN embargo on health, nutrition, and overall mortality—particularly among the country's children.

UN studies indicate that general levels of health and nutrition declined markedly after the introduction of the embargo in 1990 and before Iraq accepted the provisions of a UN program in late 1996 that allowed Iraq to sell a set quantity of oil to purchase food, medicine, and other human necessities. This situation led to substantial declines in the rates of birth, natural increase, and fertility and a noticeable increase in the death rate. Overall vital statistics in Iraq during the 1990s, however, remained above world averages and by the 21st century had begun to return to their prewar levels.

Because of Iraq's relatively low population density, the government has long promoted a policy of population growth. Although it is estimated that more than two-fifths of the population is younger than 15 years of age, the

More than two-fifths of Iraq's population is younger than age 15, but two major wars have taken a toll on young males. Joe Raedle/Getty Images

total fertility rate has declined since its peak during the late 1980s. This decline apparently resulted from the casualties of the two major wars—reaching possibly as many as a half million young and early adult men—and subsequent difficulties related to the UN embargo, as well as an overall sense of insecurity among Iraqis. For the same reasons, it is reckoned that the rate of natural increase, while still high by world standards, had dropped markedly by the mid-1990s before it likewise rebounded. Life expectancy in 2008 was estimated to be some 68 years for men and 71 years for women.

The associated hardships of the early to mid-1990s persuaded a number of Iraqis—at least those who were wealthy enough and willing to risk the wrath of the regime—to either leave the country or seek haven in the northern Kurdish region, where, thanks to international aid and a freer market, living conditions improved noticeably during the 1990s. Moreover, an estimated one to two million Iraqis—many of them unregistered refugees—fled the country to various destinations (including Iran, Syria, and Jordan) out of direct fear of government reprisal. Repatriation was slow after the demise of the Baʿthist regime.

Beyond the out-migration of a significant number of Iraqis, the major demographic trends in the country since the 1970s have been forced relocation—particularly of the Iranian population and, more recently, of the Kurds—forced ethnic homogenization, and urbanization. Eastern Iraq has traditionally formed part of a transition zone between the Arab and Persian worlds, and, until the Baʿth regime came to power in 1968, a significant number of ethnic Persians lived in the country (in the same way large numbers of ethnic Arabs reside in Iran). Between 1969 and 1980, however, they—and many Arabs whom the regime defined as Persian—were deported to Iran.

Kurds have traditionally populated the northeast, and Sunni Arabs have traditionally predominated in central Iraq. During the 1980s the Baʿth regime forcibly moved tens of thousands of Kurds from regions along the Iranian border, with many Kurds dying in the process, and subsequently relocated large numbers of Arabs to areas traditionally inhabited by Kurds, particularly in and around the city of Karkūk. Kurds in those regions have, likewise, been expelled, and many of Iraq's estimated half million internally displaced persons are Kurds. Further, the regime systematically compelled large numbers of Kurds and members of smaller ethnic groups to change their ethnic identity, forcing them to declare themselves Arabs. Those not acquiescing to this pressure faced expulsion, physical abuse, and imprisonment.

Iraqis have been slowly migrating to urban areas since the 1930s. Population mobility and urban growth have, to some extent, created a religious and cultural mix in several large cities, particularly in Baghdad. (There has been little change in the overall ethnic patterns of the country, however, except through instances of forced migration.) Many Kurds have moved either to larger towns in Kurdistan or to larger cities such as Mosul or Baghdad. Few Kurds have moved willingly to the south, where Arab Shīʿites have traditionally predominated. The latter have moved in substantial numbers to larger towns in the south or, particularly during the fighting in the 1980s, to largely Shīʿite neighbourhoods in Baghdad. Sunnis migrating from rural areas have moved mostly to areas of Baghdad with majorities of their ethnic and religious affinities.

From the mid-1970s until 1990, labour shortages drew large numbers of foreign workers, particularly Egyptians, to Iraq. At its height the number of Egyptians may have exceeded two million. Virtually all foreign workers left the country prior to the Persian Gulf War, and few, if any, have returned.

CHAPTER 3

Economy

Iraq's economy was based almost exclusively on agriculture until the 1950s, but after the 1958 revolution economic development was considerable. By 1980 Iraq had the second-largest economy in the Arab world, after Saudi Arabia, and the third largest in the Middle East and had developed a complex, centrally planned economy dominated by the state. Although the economy, particularly petroleum exports, suffered during the Iran-Iraq War—gross domestic product (GDP) actually fell in some years—the invasion of Kuwait, Iraq's subsequent defeat in the Persian Gulf War, and the UN embargo beginning in 1990 dealt a far greater blow to the financial system. Little hard evidence is available on Iraq's economy after 1990, but the best estimates available indicate that, in the year following the Persian Gulf War, GDP dropped to less than one-fourth of its previous level. Under the UN embargo the Iraqi economy languished for the next five years, and it was not until the Iraqi government implemented the UN's oil-for-food program in 1997 that Iraq's GDP again began to experience positive annual growth.

Oil production and economic development both declined after the start of the Iraq War, and the economy has continued to face serious problems, including a huge foreign debt, which has accumulated since the early 1980s largely through heavy war expenditures and continued high military spending. Other serious problems include a high rate of inflation; continuing political violence; an oil sector hampered by a shortage of replacement parts, antiquated production methods, and outdated technology; a population that has steadily moved away from agriculture; a high rate of unemployment; a seriously deteriorated infrastructure; and a private sector inexperienced in modern market practices. Following the initial phase (2003) of the Iraq War, the oil-for-food program was ended, sanctions were lifted, and civil administrators appointed by the United States took over Iraq's public sector.

ECONOMIC DEVELOPMENT

Oil revenues almost quadrupled between 1973 and 1975, and, until the outbreak of the Iran-Iraq War, this enabled the Ba'th regime to set ambitious development goals, including building industry, reducing the quantity of imported manufactured goods, expanding agriculture (though Iraq has not attained self-sufficiency), and increasing significantly its non-oil exports. Investment in infrastructure was high, notably for projects involving irrigation and water supply, roads and railways, and rural electrification. Health services were also greatly improved. War with Iran in the 1980s, however, delayed many projects and heavily damaged the country's physical

Oil production has enabled Iraq to boost its agricultural, manufacturing, and building industry development. Franc & Jean Shor/National Geographic Image Collection/Getty Images

infrastructure, especially in the southeast, where most of the fighting occurred. There was little reprieve after the war was over, as the Persian Gulf War further devastated Iraq's infrastructure and undid many of the advances of earlier decades. Attacks by the U.S.-led coalition mainly affected the communication and energy systems. When electricity failed, other systems were seriously affected, and a lack of spare parts led to further deterioration. In many parts of the country, these conditions persisted into the 21st century and were worsened by the Iraq War.

STATE CONTROL

Under the socialist Ba'th Party, the economy was dominated by the state, with strict bureaucratic controls and centralized planning. Between 1987 and 1990 the economy liberalized somewhat in an attempt to encourage private investment, particularly in small industrial and commercial enterprises, and to privatize unprofitable public assets. Entrepreneurs were encouraged to draw on funds that they had managed to transfer abroad, without threat of government reprisal or interference, and the government was able to divest itself of a number of enterprises. Yet, generally speaking, the privatization policy did not do well, mainly because elements within the bureaucracy and the security service—fearing that this course of action imperiled their interests and obviated socialist policy—objected to it but also because potential investors feared that the government might arbitrarily reverse the plan. In addition, many of the public assets offered for sale were unprofitable. After Iraq invaded Kuwait, the privatization policy died out, though private enterprise continued in the form of small- and medium-sized businesses and light industries.

AGRICULTURE, FORESTRY, AND FISHING

About one-eighth of Iraq's total area is arable, and another one-tenth is permanent pasture. A large proportion of the arable land is in the north and northeast, where rain-fed irrigation dominates and is sufficient to cultivate winter crops, mainly wheat and barley. The remainder is in the valleys of the Tigris and Euphrates rivers, where irrigation—approximately half of Iraq's arable land is irrigated—is necessary throughout the year. The cultivated area declined by about half during the 1970s, mainly because of increased soil salinity, but grew in the 1980s as a number of large reclamation projects, particularly in the central and northwestern areas, were completed. In addition, droughts in Turkey frequently reduced the amount of Euphrates water available for irrigation in the south. Although the Tigris is affected less by drought—because it has a wider drainage area, including tributaries in Iran—it has been necessary to construct several large dams throughout the river system to store water for irrigation. Careful management of the soils has been necessary to combat salinity, but the willingness of the upstream states, Turkey and Syria, to equitably divide the water of the two rivers, in spite of their own heavy demands, also has been vital to the maintenance of sufficient volume.

Agriculture traditionally accounts for one-fourth to one-third of Iraq's GDP. However, the country's agricultural sector faces many problems in addition to soil salinity and drought, including floods and siltation, which impede the efficient working of the irrigation system. A lack of access to fertilizer and agricultural spare parts after 1990 and a lengthy drought in the early 21st century led to a decrease in agricultural production.

Before the revolution of 1958, most of the agricultural land was concentrated in the hands of a few powerful landowners. The revolutionary government began a program of land reform, breaking up the large estates and distributing the land to peasant families and limiting the size of private holdings. The Ba'thist government that took over in 1968 originally encouraged public ownership and established agricultural cooperatives and collective farms, but those proved to be inefficient. After 1983 the government rented state-owned land to private concerns, with no limit on the size of holdings, and from 1987 it sold or leased all state farms. Membership in a cooperative and the use of government marketing organizations ceased to be obligatory.

The chief crops are barley, wheat, rice, vegetables, corn (maize), millet, sugarcane, sugar beets, oil seeds, fruit, fodder, tobacco, and cotton. Yields vary considerably from

Successful crop yields, including cotton, are highly dependent on the amount of rain in any given year. Ali Yussef/AFP/Getty Images

year to year, especially in areas of rain-fed cultivation. Date production—Iraq was once the world's largest date producer—was seriously damaged during the Iran-Iraq War and approached prewar levels only in the early 21st century. Animal husbandry is widely practiced, particularly among the Kurds of the northeast, and livestock products, notably milk, meat, hides, and wool, are important.

Timber resources are scarce and rather inaccessible, being situated almost entirely in the highlands and mountains of the northeast in Iraqi Kurdistan. The resources that are readily available are used almost exclusively for firewood and the production of charcoal. Limited amounts of timber are used for local industry, but most wood for industrial production (for furniture, construction, and other purposes) must be imported. Afforestation projects to supply new forest area and reduce erosion have met with limited success.

Iraq harvests both freshwater and marine fish for local consumption and also supports a modest aquaculture industry. The main freshwater fish are various species of the genus *Barbus* and carp, which are pulled from Iraqi national waters and from the Persian Gulf by Iraq's small domestic fleet. Inland bodies provide by far the largest source of fish. Various types of shad, mullet, and catfish are fished in the lakes, rivers, and streams, and fish farms mostly provide varieties of carp. There is no industrial fish-processing sector, and most fish is consumed fresh by the domestic market. Fishing contributes only a tiny fraction to GDP.

RESOURCES AND POWER

Iraq is endowed with a number of important natural resources, including petroleum—its reserves are among the world's largest—and natural gas. Iraq also has what are believed to be some of the world's largest rock sulfur reserves. Electricity, which is produced largely by thermal plants and to a lesser extent through hydroelectricity, fails to meet demand.

Petroleum

Petroleum is Iraq's most valuable mineral. The country has the world's second-largest known reserves and, before the Iran-Iraq War, was the second-largest oil-exporting state. Oil production contributes the largest single portion to GDP and constitutes almost all of Iraq's foreign exchange. Iraq is a founding member of the Organization of Petroleum Exporting Countries (OPEC), but disagreements over production quotas and world oil prices have often led Iraq into conflict with other members.

Oil was first discovered in Iraq in 1927 near Karkūk by the foreign-owned Turkish Petroleum Company, which was renamed the Iraq Petroleum Company (IPC) in 1929. Finds at Mosul and Al-Baṣrah followed, and several new fields were discovered and put into production in the 1940s and '50s. New fields continue to be discovered and developed.

The IPC was nationalized in 1972, as were all foreign-owned oil companies by 1975, and all facets of Iraq's oil industry were thereafter controlled by the government through the Iraq National Oil Company and its subsidiaries. During the war with Iran, production and distribution facilities were badly damaged, and after Iraq's invasion of Kuwait—which was itself partly prompted by disagreements over production quotas and disputes over oil field rights—the UN embargo on Iraq halted all exports. Under the embargo Iraq exported little or no oil until the oil-for-food program was implemented. By the early 21st century, oil production and exports had risen to roughly three-fourths of the levels achieved prior to the Persian Gulf War. Oil production rebounded slowly following the initial phase of the Iraq War.

Oil Pipelines

Because Iraq has such a short coastline, it has depended heavily on transnational pipelines to export its oil. This need has been compounded by the fact that Iraq's narrow coastline is adjacent to that of Iran, a country with which Iraq frequently has had strained relations. Originally (1937–48) oil from the northern fields (mainly Karkūk) was pumped to the Mediterranean Sea through Haifa, Palestine (now in Israel), a practice that the Iraqis abandoned with the establishment of the Jewish state. Soon thereafter pipelines to the Mediterranean were built to Bāniyās, Syria, and through Syria to Tripoli, Lebanon. In 1977 a large pipeline was completed to the Turkish Mediterranean coast at Ceyhan. When the first Turkish line was completed, Iraq ceased using the Syrian pipelines and relied on the outlet through Turkey and on new terminals on the Persian Gulf (although export through Syria briefly resumed in the early 1980s). By 1979 Iraq had three gulf terminals—Mīnā' al-Bakr, Khawr al-Amaya, and Khawr al-Zubayr—all of which were damaged during one or the other of Iraq's recent wars. In 1985 Iraq constructed a new pipeline that fed into the Petroline (in Saudi Arabia), which terminated at the Red Sea port of Yanbu'. In 1988 that line was replaced with a new one, but it never reached full capacity and was shut down, along with all other Iraqi oil outlets, following Iraq's invasion of Kuwait.

In December 1996 the Turkish pipeline was reopened under the oil-for-food program. Later the gulf terminal of Mīnā' al-Bakr also was revived, and in 1998 repairs were begun on the Syrian pipeline. Following the start of the Iraq War in 2003, Iraq's pipelines were subjected to numerous acts of sabotage by guerrilla forces.

Other Minerals and Energy

Exploitation of other minerals has lagged far behind that of oil and natural gas. It seems likely that Iraq has a good range of these untapped resources. Huge rock sulfur reserves—estimated to be among the largest in the world—are exploited at Mishraq, near Mosul, and in the early 1980s phosphate production began at 'Akāshāt, near the Syrian border. The phosphates are used in a large fertilizer plant at Al-Qā'im. Lesser quantities of salt and steel are produced, and construction materials, including stone and gypsum (from which cement is produced), are plentiful.

Iraq's electrical production fails to meet its needs. Energy rationing is pervasive, and mandatory power outages are practiced throughout the country. This is largely because of damage by the Persian Gulf War, which destroyed the bulk of the country's power grid, including more than four-fifths of its power stations and a large part of its distribution facilities. In spite of a shortage of spare parts, Iraq was able—largely through cannibalizing equipment—to reconstruct roughly three-fourths of its national grid by 1992. By the end of the decade, however, this level of energy production had decreased, in part as a result of a reduced level of hydroelectric generation caused by drought but also because there continued to be a lack of replacements for aging components. Damage from the Iraq War has been less severe, but energy production remains below installed capacity.

The bulk of electricity generation is by thermal plants. Even in the best of times—in spite of the many dams on Iraq's rivers—the hydroelectricity produced is below installed capacity. The largest hydroelectric plants are at the Ṣaddām Dam on the Tigris, the Dokan Dam on the Little Zab River, the Darbandikhan Dam on the Diyālā in eastern Kurdistan, and the Sāmarrā' Dam on Lake Al-Tharthār. A Chinese company completed a new plant near Karkūk in 2000 and has contracted to repair other facilities.

MANUFACTURING

The manufacturing sector developed rapidly after the mid-1970s, when government policy shifted toward heavy industrialization and import substitution. Iraq's program received assistance from many countries, particularly from the former Soviet Union. The state generally has controlled all heavy manufacturing, the oil sector, power production, and the infrastructure, although private investment in manufacturing was at times encouraged. Until 1980 most heavy manufacturing was greatly subsidized and made little economic sense, but it brought prestige for the Baʿth regime and later, during the Iran-Iraq War, served as a basis for the country's massive military buildup. Petrochemical and iron and steel plants were built at Khawr al-Zubayr, and petrochemical production and oil refining were greatly expanded both at Al-Baṣrah and at Al-Musayyib, 40 miles (65 km) south of Baghdad, which was designated as the site of an enormous integrated industrial complex. In addition, a wide range of industrial activities were started up, some of which were boosted by the Iran-Iraq War, notably aluminum smelting and the production of tractors, electrical goods, telephone cables, and tires. Petrochemical products for export also were expanded and diversified to include liquefied natural gas, bitumen, detergents, and a range of fertilizers.

The combined results of the Iran-Iraq War, both the Persian Gulf War and the Iraq War, and, most of all, the UN embargo eroded Iraq's manufacturing capacity. Within its first two years, the embargo had cut manufacturing—which was already well below its highs of the early 1980s—by more than half. After 1997, however, there was an increase in manufacturing output, in both the public and the private sectors, as replacement parts and government credit became available. By the end of the decade, large numbers of products long unavailable to consumers were once again on the market, and almost all the factories that were operating before the imposition

Although considerably depleted by wars and the UN embargo, Iraq's manufacturing began to resume production toward the end of the 1990s. Ahmad Al-Rubaye/AFP/Getty Images

of the embargo had resumed production, albeit at somewhat lower levels.

FINANCE

All banks and insurance companies were nationalized in 1964. The Central Bank of Iraq (founded in 1947 and one of the first central banks in the Arab world) has the sole right to issue the dinar, the national currency. The Rafidain Bank (1941) is the oldest commercial bank, but in 1988 the state founded a second commercial bank, the Rashid (Rasheed) Bank. There are also three state-owned specialized banks: the Agricultural Co-operative Bank (1936), the Industrial Bank (1940), and the Real Estate Bank (1949). Beginning in 1991 the government authorized private banks to operate, but only under the strict supervision of the central bank. The Baghdad Stock Exchange opened in 1992.

By 2004, after three major wars and years of international isolation, the national accounts were in disarray, and the country was saddled with an enormous national debt. At the end of the Persian Gulf War, the value of the formerly sound dinar plummeted in the face of rampant inflation. The UN embargo made it difficult for Iraqi banks to operate outside the country, and, under UN auspices, numerous Iraqi assets and accounts, including those in Iraq's financial institutions, were frozen and later seized by host governments in order to pay the country's numerous outstanding debts. Under the stipulations of the oil-for-food program, all revenues derived from the export of Iraqi oil were placed in escrow and supervised by the international community. After the initial phase of the Iraq War, the United States sought ways to refinance or forgive portions of the country's debt.

Although Iraqi exports centre chiefly on oil, dates are one of the country's agricultural exports. Ali Yussef/AFP/Getty Images

TRADE

Before the UN embargo, Iraq was a heavy importer. The chief imports included military ordnance, vehicles, industrial and electrical goods, textiles and clothing, and construction materials. About one-fourth of import spending was on foodstuffs. Exports—though dominated by oil, which accounted for nearly all of total export value—were relatively diverse and included such items as dates, cotton, wool, animal products, and fertilizers. All legal international trade ground to a virtual halt following the invasion of Kuwait and the imposition of the embargo. Only with the start of the oil-for-food program did Iraq again begin to engage in international trade—albeit under strict UN supervision. Beginning in 2002 the UN eased trade restrictions to allow a broader range of imports, and the following year the embargo was lifted. Foodstuffs are still imported in large quantities, as are consumer goods of all types. Exports now consist mostly of petroleum and petroleum products, which are shipped to a number of countries, including the United States, Italy, France, and Spain. Iraq is a member of the Arab Common Market.

SERVICES

Like every other part of the economy, the service sector suffered during the embargo. Retail sales fell off as unemployment rose and as the buying power of the dinar sharply decreased. A large portion of every Iraqi's salary—even among the once-thriving middle class—went to such necessities as food and shelter. Iraq's somewhat isolated geographic location and its decades of near perpetual political instability have seriously impeded the possibility that tourism, in spite of the country's deep historical wealth, might soon become a major source of national income. The only sector of the service economy that consistently thrived throughout the embargo was the construction industry. The government invested a large portion of its limited resources in repairing the damage of the Persian Gulf War (particularly in and around Baghdad) and to constructing grandiose monuments and palaces for the regime and its leader, Ṣaddām Ḥussein.

LABOUR AND TAXATION

Labour laws enacted following the revolution offer protection to employees, including minimum wages and unemployment benefits. Traditionally, there have also been benefits for maternity, old age, and illness. It is unclear how these measures have been honoured since the early 1990s. Trade unions were legalized in 1936, but their effectiveness was limited by government and Baʿth Party control. Iraq's only labour organization is the General Federation of Trade Unions (GFTU), established in 1987, which is affiliated with the International Confederation of Arab Trade Unions and the World Federation of Trade Unions. Under the Baʿth government, workers in the private sector were allowed to join only local unions associated with the GFTU, which in reality was closely tied to, and controlled by, the party and was largely a vehicle for Baʿthist ideology. Collective bargaining traditionally has not been practiced, and workers effectively have been barred from striking. Under labour laws adopted in that period, children younger than 14 years of age are allowed to work only in small family businesses, and those younger than 18 may work only a limited number of hours. In reality, however, the extreme economic situation that began in the 1990s forced many children to enter the workforce. Unemployment and underemployment were extremely high during the 1990s—a considerable change for a country that had traditionally imported labour—and continued into the 21st century. As in many Islamic countries, the standard workweek is Sunday through Thursday, but many labourers toil six or seven days per week, some at more than one job.

Since the oil boom of the 1970s, the overwhelming majority of government revenue has been generated by the export and sale of petroleum. As a consequence, Iraq's system of taxation is only poorly developed. The government scrambled to find new sources of revenue after the UN embargo was imposed in 1990, but these were few and consisted largely of sporadic taxation, property confiscation (mainly from enemies of the regime), and the government monopoly over export trade—largely clandestine shipments of oil—in defiance of the embargo. After the oil-for-food program was established, oil revenues were held in escrow by the UN. Following the start of the Iraq War, the country relied on international aid to augment income from oil exports.

TRANSPORTATION AND TELECOMMUNICATIONS

Iraq's transport system encompasses all kinds of travel, both ancient and contemporary. In some desert and mountain regions, the inhabitants still rely on camels, horses, and donkeys. In spite of the disruption caused by events since 1980, the country's transportation systems are, by the standards of the region, reasonably high.

The road network has been markedly improved since the 1950s, and more than four-fifths of the road mileage is paved. There are good road links with neighbouring countries, particularly with Kuwait and Jordan. The most extensive road network is in central and southern Iraq.

The rail system is controlled by Iraqi Republic Railways. The main lines include a metre-gauge line from Baghdad to Karkūk and Arbīl and a standard-gauge line from Baghdad to Mosul and Turkey. To the south a standard-gauge line from Baghdad reaches Al-Baṣrah and Umm Qaṣr. A line links Iraq with the Syrian railway system. International rail service was interrupted during the political turmoil of the 1980s and was not reestablished with Syria until 2000 or with Turkey until 2001.

Rivers, lakes, and channels have long been used for local transport. For large vessels, river navigation is difficult because of flooding, shifting canals, and shallows. Nevertheless, the Tigris is navigable by steamers to Baghdad, and smaller craft can travel upstream to Mosul. Navigation of the Euphrates is confined to small craft and large rafts that carry goods downstream. Oceangoing ships can reach Al-Baṣrah, 85 miles (135 km) upstream on the Shatt al-Arab, only through regular dredging. Until the Iran-Iraq War, Al-Baṣrah handled the great bulk of Iraq's trade, but since then—and even more so since 1996—Umm Qaṣr has been developed as an alternative port. It is linked with Al-Zubayr, 30 miles (50 km) inland, via the canalized Khawr al-Zubayr. Much Iraqi trade also passes through the Jordanian port of Al-ʿAqabah, from which goods are carried overland by truck. Since 1999 merchandise also has come through Syria's port city of Latakia.

The national airline, Iraqi Airways, was founded in 1945, and domestic air traffic was relatively light at the outbreak of the Persian Gulf War. A ban on flights south of latitude 32° N (since 1996, 33° N) and north of 36° N (the so-called "no-fly zones") that was established after the war forced domestic air traffic virtually to cease until late 2000. There are international airports at Baghdad (the country's main point of entry) and Al-Baṣrah, as well as four regional airports and several large military fields.

Iraq's telecommunication network, once one of the best in the region, was heavily damaged during the Persian Gulf War and was further degraded in 2003. The network has been repaired only partially and has suffered from inadequate maintenance and a chronic lack of spare parts. Services that are available are of a poor quality. There are approximately three main telephone lines per hundred residents and only slightly greater access to television, with less than one set per 10 residents. About one-fifth of the population has regular access to radio. All television and radio broadcast stations were either directly or indirectly controlled by the government, but after 2003 restrictions were dropped, and television service via satellite boomed. Cellular telephone service, unavailable under the Ba'th government, is now accessible in urban areas, and Internet access is available to a much wider audience.

CHAPTER 4

Government and Society

From 1968 to 2003 Iraq was ruled by the Ba'th (Arabic: "Renaissance") Party. Under a provisional constitution adopted by the party in 1970, Iraq was confirmed as a republic, with legislative power theoretically vested in an elected legislature but also in the party-run Revolutionary Command Council (RCC), without whose approval no law could be promulgated. Executive power rested with the president, who also served as the chairman of the RCC, supervised the cabinet ministers, and ostensibly reported to the RCC. Judicial power was also, in theory, vested in an independent judiciary. The political system, however, operated with little reference to constitutional provisions,

Between 1979 and 2003, Pres. Ṣaddām Ḥussein effectively exerted unrestricted control. Thomas Hartwell/Time & Life Pictures/Getty Images

and from 1979 to 2003 President Ṣaddām Ḥussein wielded virtually unlimited power.

Following the overthrow of the Ba'th government in 2003, the United States and its coalition allies established the Coalition Provisional Authority (CPA), headed by a senior American diplomat. In July the CPA appointed the 25-member Iraqi Governing Council (IGC), which assumed limited governing functions. The IGC approved an interim constitution in March 2004, and a permanent constitution was approved by a national plebiscite in October 2005. This document established Iraq as a federal state in which limited authority—over matters such as defense, foreign affairs, and customs regulations—was vested in the national government. A variety of issues (e.g., general planning, education, and health care) are shared competencies, and other issues are treated at the discretion of the district and regional constituencies.

The constitution is in many ways the framework for a fairly typical parliamentary democracy. The president is the head of state, the prime minister is the head of government, and the constitution provides for two deliberative bodies, the Council of Representatives (Majlis al-Nawwāb) and the Council of Union (Majlis al-Ittiḥād). The judiciary is free and independent of the executive and the legislature.

The president, who is nominated by the Council of Representatives and who is limited to two four-year terms, holds what is largely a ceremonial position. The head of state presides over state ceremonies, receives ambassadors, endorses treaties and laws, and awards medals and honours. The president also calls upon the leading party in legislative elections to form a government (the executive), which consists of the prime minister and the cabinet and which, in turn, must seek the approval of the Council of Representatives to assume power. The executive is responsible for setting policy and for the day-to-day running of the government. The executive also may propose legislation to the Council of Representatives.

The Council of Representatives does not have a set number of seats but is based on a formula of one representative for every 100,000 citizens. Ministers serve four-year terms and sit in session for eight months per year. The council's functions include enacting federal laws, monitoring the performance of the prime minister and the president, ratifying foreign treaties, and approving appointments. In addition, it has the authority to declare war.

The constitution is very brief on the issue of the Council of Union, the structure, duties, and powers of which apparently will be left to later legislation. The constitution only notes that this body will include representatives of the regions and governorates, suggesting that it will likely take the form of an upper house.

Ba'th Party

The Ba'th Party (in full, Arab Socialist Ba'th Party, or Arab Socialist Renaissance Party; Arabic: Ḥizb al-Ba'th al-'Arabī al-Ishtirākī) is an Arab political party advocating the formation of a single Arab socialist nation. It has branches in many Middle Eastern countries and was the ruling party in Syria from 1963 and in Iraq from 1968 to 2003.

The Ba'th Party was founded in 1943 in Damascus by Michel 'Aflaq and Ṣalaḥ al-Dīn al-Bīṭār, adopted its constitution in 1947, and in 1953 merged with the Syrian Socialist Party to form the Arab Socialist Ba'th ("Renaissance") Party. The Ba'th Party espoused nonalignment and opposition to imperialism and colonialism, took inspiration from what it considered the positive values of Islam, and attempted to ignore or transcend class divisions. Its structure was highly centralized and authoritarian.

The Syrian Ba'thists took power in 1963, but factionalism between "progressives" and "nationalists" was severe until 1970, when Ḥafiz al-Assad of the "nationalists" secured control. In Iraq the Ba'thists took power briefly in 1963 and regained it in 1968, after which the party's power became concentrated under Iraqi leader Ṣaddām Ḥussein. Differences between the Iraqi and Syrian wings of the Ba'th Party precluded unification of the two countries. Within both countries the Ba'thists formed fronts with smaller parties, including at times the communists. In Syria the main internal threat to Ba'th hegemony stemmed from the Muslim Brotherhood, while in Iraq Kurdish and Shī'ite opposition was endemic. The Iraqi branch of the party was toppled in 2003 as a result of the Iraq War.

LOCAL GOVERNMENT

Iraq is divided for administrative purposes into *muḥāfaẓāt* (governorates), several of which constitute the Kurdish Autonomous Region. Each governorate has a governor, or *muḥāfiẓ*, appointed by the president. The governorates are in turn divided into *aqḍiyyah* (districts), headed by district officers, and each district is divided into *nāḥiyāt* (tracts), headed by directors. Towns and cities have their own municipal councils, each of which is directed by a mayor. Baghdad has special status and its own governor. The Kurdish Autonomous Region was formed by government decree in 1974, but in reality it attained autonomy only with the help of coalition forces following the Persian Gulf War. It is governed by an elected legislative council. The Kurdish Region was ratified under the 2005 constitution, which also authorizes the establishment of future regions in other parts of Iraq as part of a federal state.

JUSTICE

The Supreme Judicial Council administers judicial affairs in Iraq. It nominates the justices of the Supreme Court, the national prosecutor, and other high judicial officials for approval by the Council of Representatives. Members of the Supreme Court are required to be experts in civil law and Muslim canon law and are appointed by two-thirds majority of the legislature. In addition to interpreting the constitution and adjudicating legal issues at the national level, the Supreme Court also settles disputes over legal issues between national government and lower jurisdictions. During the Baʿth era the judiciary was generally bypassed, and the regime instituted a wide variety of exceptional courts whose authority circumvented the constitution. The establishment of such courts is clearly proscribed under the 2005 constitution. All additional courts are to be established by due process of law.

POLITICAL PROCESS

The Baʿth Party was a self-styled socialist and Arab nationalist party once connected with the ruling Baʿth Party in Syria, although the two parties were often at odds. After the Baʿth Party came to power, Iraq became effectively a one-party state, with all governing institutions nominally espousing the Baʿth ideology. In 1973 the Iraqi Communist Party (ICP) agreed to join a Baʿth-dominated National Progressive Front, and in 1974 a group of Kurdish political parties, including the Kurdish Democratic Party (KDP), joined. In 1979, after the ICP had suffered serious disagreements with the Baʿth leadership and a bloody purge, it left the Front, and it was subsequently outlawed by the government. In addition to the ICP, several other opposition parties were outlawed by the Baʿth. The best known among them are the KDP, the Patriotic Union of Kurdistan (PUK), and two religious Shīʿite parties: the Daʿwah ("Call") Islamic Party and the Supreme Council of the Islamic Revolution in Iraq. Another group, the Iraqi National Congress, received strong, albeit intermittent, support of the U.S. government during the 1990s. All operated outside Iraq or in areas of the country not under government control.

Following the Persian Gulf War, the KDP and the PUK, although often at odds with one another, operated in the Kurdish Autonomous Region with relative freedom and remained largely unhindered by the government. In the rest of Iraq, however, isolation and the UN embargo further consolidated power in the hands of the government. Following the overthrow of the Baʿthists in 2003, a number of small political parties arose, and the major expatriate parties resumed operations domestically.

SECURITY

The Iraqi armed forces have often intervened in the country's political life. There were numerous military coups between 1936 and 1968, and though the Baʿth regime depended heavily on military support for its survival, its mistrust of the military caused it to distance the armed forces from politics. There were frequent purges of the officer corps to root out those suspected of disloyalty, and security duties were divided between a complex network of military, paramilitary, and intelligence services, many of which reported directly to the president and all of which were commanded by individuals whose allegiance to him was without question.

Although the Ba'th regime heavily relied on military assistance to survive, its wariness of the military was a source of great tension. Karim Sahib/AFP/Getty Images

In the 1970s Iraq began a systematic buildup of its armed forces, and by 1990 it had the most powerful army in the Arab world—and perhaps the fourth or fifth largest in the world. More than one million soldiers were under arms and had access to a plentiful supply of sophisticated weaponry. During the Persian Gulf War, the army suffered heavy losses in troops and matériel, and afterward it was trimmed to roughly one-third of its previous size. Remaining units were badly equipped, morale was low, and desertion was common. By the early 21st century, the regular army could still suppress internal revolts but was no match for the armies of neighbouring countries.

Iraq had a small but growing navy that was designed primarily for river and coastal defense. A once larger naval force was completely paralyzed by Iranian superiority at sea during the Iran-Iraq War and was virtually destroyed during the Persian Gulf War. New ships purchased abroad never arrived owing to the UN embargo, under which Iraq was not allowed to rebuild naval forces. The Iraqi air force was formerly large and well-equipped, but roughly half of its combat aircraft either were destroyed or were flown into hiding (many to Iran, which has since refused to return them) during the Persian Gulf War. Half of Iraq's remaining aircraft were rendered inoperable owing to poor maintenance and a lack of spare components during the 1990s. However, Iraq devoted significant resources to air defense.

Under Ṣaddām Ḥussein, major military programs centred on stockpiling chemical and biological weapons, developing a nuclear weapons program (or obtaining completed nuclear weapons), and creating a missile system capable of delivering chemical, biological, and nuclear warheads a distance of 600 to 800 miles (950 to 1,300 km). After the Persian Gulf War, the international community attempted to compel Iraq to stop developing such weapons, and reports that the country continued to stockpile those weapons and obtain associated matériel and technology served as the casus belli for the Iraq War. After the overthrow of the Ba'thists, members of paramilitary groups fled into hiding, and the CPA disbanded the armed forces. A new army of much smaller dimensions was recruited soon after.

HEALTH AND WELFARE

Between 1958 and 1991 health care was free, welfare services were expanded, and considerable sums were invested in housing for the poor and for improvements to domestic water and electrical services. Almost all medical facilities were controlled by the government, and most physicians were (and still are) employed by the Ministry of Health. Shortages of medical personnel were felt only in rural areas. Cities and towns had good hospitals, and clinics and dispensaries served most rural areas. Still, Iraq had a high incidence of infectious diseases such as malaria and typhoid, caused by rural water supplies largely contaminated by periodic flooding. Substantial progress, however, was made in controlling malaria.

The Persian Gulf War greatly damaged components of the infrastructure, which had the immediate effect of higher rates of mortality and increased instances of malnutrition (especially among young children). However, by 1997 overall levels of health care had begun to increase as the oil-for-food program began to generate revenue for food and medicine. By the early 21st century, medical care, though no longer free, was still affordable for most

Even after the destruction caused by the Persian Gulf War, health and medical care became much more available than it had been at the start of the UN embargo. Marco Di Lauro/Getty Images

citizens and was much more readily available than it had been since the start of the embargo. Shortages remained, especially of medicine, potable water, and trained medical staff.

Health care in most parts of the Kurdish Autonomous Region actually improved during the 1990s, and child mortality fell significantly. Malnutrition was much less common than in the remainder of Iraq, and by the 21st century potable water was available to four-fifths of the rural population (up from three-fifths in the mid-1990s). After 2003 the health care system relied heavily on donations from abroad and the efforts of international aid organizations.

HOUSING

The availability of adequate housing remained a problem in Iraq at the beginning of the 21st century. This was partly attributable to the major demographic shifts that had occurred in preceding decades, with large numbers of Shīʿites fleeing the south to overcrowded Baghdad and large groups of Kurds, Turkmens, and Assyrians being displaced by government policy in the north. Access to adequate water, electricity, and sanitation remained a problem both for new housing constructions and for existing residences. Many new immigrants to the city have been forced to reside in urban slums lacking all modern conveniences, and internally displaced persons in the north have had to live for times in tents, shantytowns, and other temporary residences.

Domestic architecture shows distinct regional variations, but the basic house types are similar to those of neighbouring countries. Mud brick is common throughout the south, while more stone is used in the north. Some of the larger villages are surrounded by mud-brick walls.

Distinctive reed houses with their barrel-vaulted roofs are traditional architecture in Iraq's marsh areas. AFP/Getty Images

The traditional reed houses of the marsh dwellers of the Al-ʿAmārah area, with their remarkable barrel-vaulted roofs, are unique to Iraq.

EDUCATION

The Ministry of Education and the Ministry of Higher Education and Scientific Research have been responsible for the rapid expansion of education since the 1958 revolution. The number of qualified scientists, administrators, technicians, and skilled workers in Iraq traditionally has been among the highest in the Middle East. Education at all levels is funded by the state. Primary education (ages 6 to 12) is compulsory, and secondary education (ages 12 to 18) is widely available. At one time many Iraqi students went abroad, particularly to the United States and Europe, for university and graduate training, but this became rare following the Persian Gulf War. Iraqi girls have also been afforded good opportunities in education, and at times the rate of female university graduates has exceeded that of males.

Beginning in the early 1990s, however, enrollment, for both boys and girls, fell considerably at all levels as many were forced to leave school and enter the workforce. Moreover, lacking access to the latest texts and equipment, Iraqi schools slowly fell behind those of other countries in the region in terms of the quality of education they offered. The educational system had formerly been highly politicized, and, following the fall of the Ba'th Party, an entirely new approach was encouraged by the CPA and the Iraqi Governing Council.

CHAPTER 5

Cultural Life

The fundamental cultural milieu of Iraq is both Islamic and Arab and shares many of the customs and traditions of the Arab world as a whole. Within Iraq, however, there is rich cultural diversity. A variety of peoples were embraced by Iraq when it was carved out of the Ottoman Empire in 1920. These included the nomadic tribes of the arid south and west (related to the Bedouin of neighbouring states), the peasant farmers of central Iraq, the marsh dwellers of the south, the dryland cultivators of the northeast, and the mountain herders of Kurdistan. Adaptations to these contrasting environments have generated a mosaic of distinctive regional cultures manifested in folk customs, food, dress, and domestic architecture. Such regional differences are reinforced by the ethno-religious contrasts between Kurds and Arabs and by the fundamental division within Islam between Shīʿites and Sunnis. These divisions are less marked than they were in the early 20th century but are still evident in the human geography of Iraq.

Daily Life and Social Customs

War always ravages daily life, and, following the start of the Iraq War, there were few aspects of daily social interaction that were unaffected by the shortages of water and electricity, damaged infrastructure, soaring unemployment, collapse of government facilities, or violence of postwar guerrilla action. In broader terms, however, over the course of the 20th century, one development was evident: rapid urban growth accelerated social change in Iraq as a higher proportion of the population was exposed to modern, largely Westernized, lifestyles. Traditional social relationships, in which the family, the extended family, and the tribe are the prime focus, have remained fundamentally important in rural areas but are under pressure in the towns. Alcoholic beverages and Western-style entertainment have become freely available, a circumstance much deplored by devout Muslims. Although the number of Muslims in Iraq embracing a fundamentalist interpretation of Islam has grown—as it has elsewhere in the Middle East—Islamic extremism has not presented a major social or political problem, given the nature of the former regime. The role of women has been changing, with a higher proportion participating in the labour force in spite of encouragement from the government to stay at home and raise large families.

Although Iraqis generally are a religious and conservative people, there are strong secular tendencies in the country. This is reflected in the dress, which, while conservative by Western standards (short or revealing clothes for men or women are considered inappropriate), is quite relaxed by the standards of the region, particularly compared with neighbouring Saudi Arabia and the Persian Gulf states. Men will frequently wear Western-style suits or, in more casual surroundings, the long shirtlike *thawb*. The traditional chador and veil, the *ḥijāb*, is common among conservative women—especially those from rural areas—but Western attire is also common.

Iraqi cuisine mirrors that of Syria and Lebanon, with strong influences from the culinary traditions of Turkey and Iran. As in other parts of the Middle East, chicken and lamb are favourite meats and are often marinated with garlic, lemon, and spices and grilled over charcoal. Flatbread is a staple that is served at every meal with a variety of dips, cheeses, olives, and jams. Fruits and vegetables are also staples, particularly the renowned Iraqi dates, which are plentiful, sweet, and

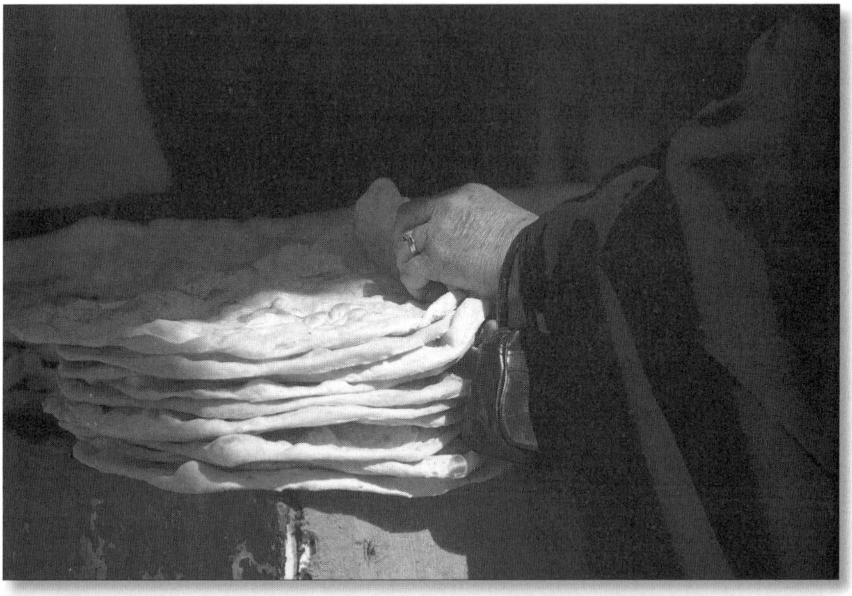

A staple at Iraqi meals, flatbread is usually served with dips, cheeses, and olives. Filippo Monteforte/AFP/Getty Images

delicious and, along with coffee, are served at the end of almost every meal.

THE ARTS

In spite of Iraq's political hardships, literary and artistic pursuits flourish, especially in Baghdad, where Western artistic traditions—including ballet, theatre, and modern art—are juxtaposed with more traditional Middle Eastern forms of artistic expression. Poetry thrives in Iraq: 20-century Iraqi poets, such as Muḥammad Mahdī al-Jawāhirī, Nāzik al-Malā'ika (one of the Arab world's most prominent woman poets), Badr Shākir al-Sayyāb, and 'Abd al-Wahhāb al-Bayatī, are known throughout the Arabic-speaking world. Iraqi painters and sculptors are among the best in the Middle East, and some of them, such as Ismā'īl Fattāḥ Turk,

Khālid al-Raḥḥāl, and Muḥammad Ghanī, have become world renowned. The Ministry of Culture and Information has endeavoured to preserve traditional arts and crafts such as leatherworking, copper working, and carpet making.

Culture continues to thrive in Iraq, as evidenced by the popularity of poets such as 'Abd al-Wahhāb al-Bayatī. Mohamad Al Sehety/AFP/Getty Images

From 1969 the Ba'th Party made a concentrated effort to create a culture designed to establish a new national identity that reflected the territorial roots of the Iraqi people. Independent Iraqi artists and intellectuals had started a trend similar to this in the 1950s, and Iraq's leader during the latter part of that decade and in the early 1960s, General 'Abd al-Karīm Qāsim, encouraged it during his rule. The Ba'th regime, however, assumed full control of the program and took it to its zenith: playwrights, novelists, film producers, poets, and sculptors were encouraged to demonstrate the historical and cultural connection between the modern Iraqi people and the ancient peoples and civilizations of Mesopotamia. Archaeological museums were built in every governorate, and a European-style version of Babylon was built on its ancient ruins. A plethora of "territorial" cultural festivals were introduced, the most important of which was the Babylon International Festival, held in September in a reconstructed Hellenistic theatre on the ancient city site.

'Abd al-Wahhāb al-Bayatī

(b. 1926, Baghdad, Iraq—d. Aug. 3, 1999, Damascus, Syria)

'Abd al-Wahhāb al-Bayatī was an Iraqi modernist poet who was a pioneer in the use of free verse rather than classical Arabic poetic forms. Although al-Bayatī spent a decade (1980–90) as Iraq's cultural attaché to Spain, his leftist political views and outspoken opposition to the Iraqi government caused him to spend most of his life in self-imposed exile. He was stripped of his citizenship in 1995, but his work—comprising more than 20 volumes of poetry—was never officially banned in Iraq.

The regime also encouraged a return to tribal values and affinities and supported a return to Islamic tradition and law. Every aspect of this cultural rebirth, of course, was deeply penetrated by Ṣaddām's personality cult (not unlike the *personalismo* of Latin America). Images of the ruler, whether statues, photos, or portraits (his likeness adorned the national currency), were omnipresent, and his name was invoked at every public ceremony.

CULTURAL INSTITUTIONS

The National Museum of Iraq (founded 1923), with its collection of antiquities, and the National Library (1961) are located in Baghdad. The city also has some fine buildings from the golden age of 'Abbāsid architecture in the 8th and 9th centuries and from the various Ottoman periods. In the 1970s the government made an effort to renovate some of Baghdad's historical buildings and even whole streets, with partial success. A number of renowned archaeological sites are located in Iraq, and artifacts from these sites are displayed in excellent museums such as the national museum and the Mosul Museum (1951). In less troubled times more than a million tourists would visit Iraq each year, many of them Shīʿites visiting revered shrines at Karbalāʾ and Al-Najaf. Since the start of the international embargo, tourism has almost completely stopped. After 1998 Iranian pilgrims were again allowed into the Shīʿite holy cities, and since 2003 virtually all limits have been removed from such travel.

National Museum of Iraq

The National Museum of Iraq, founded in 1923 and located in Baghdad, features Iraqi art and artifacts dating from the Stone Age civilization of the Fertile Crescent to the Middle Ages. Following World War I, archaeologists from Europe and the United States began several excavations throughout Iraq. To keep those finds

The National Museum of Iraq features art from ancient Assyrian, Sumerian, Babylonian, Akkadian, and Chaldean civilizations. AFP/Getty Images

from leaving Iraq, Gertrude Bell, a British intelligence agent, archaeologist, and director of antiquities in Iraq, began collecting the artifacts in a government building in Baghdad. The Iraqi government moved the collection to a new building in 1926 and established the Baghdad Antiquities Museum, with Bell as its director. In 1966 the collection was moved again, to a two-story, 484,375-square-foot (45,000-square-metre) building in Baghdad's Al-Ṣāliḥiyyah neighbourhood in Al-Karkh district on the east side of the Tigris River. With this move the name of the museum was changed to the National Museum of Iraq. About 3,000 items were looted from the museum following the U.S.-led invasion of Iraq in 2003. This sparked an international effort by law enforcement officials and archaeologists to catalogue and retrieve the missing items. In February 2009 the museum reopened after being closed for some six years. At that time it was estimated that only about one-fourth of the stolen items had been recovered.

The collections of the National Museum of Iraq include art and artifacts from ancient Sumerian, Babylonian, Akkadian, Assyrian, and Chaldean civilizations. The museum also has galleries devoted to collections of both pre-Islamic and Islamic Arabian art and artifacts. Of its many noteworthy collections, the Nimrud gold collection—which features gold jewelry and figures of precious stone that date to the 9th century BCE—and the collection of stone carvings and cuneiform tablets from Uruk are exceptional. The Uruk treasures date to between 3500 and 3000 BCE.

SPORTS AND RECREATION

As it is in most other Arab countries, football (soccer) is Iraq's national passion. It became increasingly popular as a means of coping with the political and economic turmoil after 1980. A popular venue in Baghdad is Al-Sha'b ("People's") Stadium, where throngs of Iraqis wait outside the gates even after the stadium has filled. Millions more watch via television throughout the country. In 2006 the

Passions run high when it comes to Iraqi football (soccer), the country's most popular sport. Ahmad Al-Rubaye/AFP/Getty Images

national football team participated in the Asian Cup finals for the first time in more than two decades, and in 2007 they won the title.

The Iraqi National Olympic Committee (INOC) was formed in 1948, and later that year the country made its Olympic debut in London. However, Iraq did not return to Olympic competition until the 1960 Summer Games, when it won its first medal (in weight lifting). Since missing the 1972 and 1976 Games, Iraqi athletes have consistently attended the Olympics, but they have not competed at the Winter Games.

Under the Ba'th Party, sports were highly politicized. 'Udayy Ḥussein, one of Ṣaddām's sons, was both the chairman of the INOC and the president of the Iraqi Football Federation. Iraq was suspended from the Olympic Council of Asia (OCA) after the OCA president was killed by Iraqi troops during the Persian Gulf War. The country did not attend the Pan-Arab Games in 1992 or in 1997, and Kuwait and Saudi Arabia at times boycotted games in which Iraq participated.

MEDIA AND PUBLISHING

The media in Iraq are well developed, though they have traditionally been conservative and conformist in nature. There are a national television service and a number of regional television stations, including a Kurdish-language station. The leading Arabic newspapers are *Al-Thawrah* ("The Revolution"), *Al-'Irāq*, and *Al-Jumhūriyyah* ("The Republic"), and a variety of other newspapers and periodicals are published. Most communications media were owned and fully controlled by the government, but after the start of the Iraq War in 2003, an explosion of new publications of all types occurred, and diverse political views began to be aired.

HISTORY

CHAPTER 6

The name Iraq is widely used in the medieval Arabic sources for the area in the centre and south of the modern republic as a geographic rather than a political term, implying no precise boundaries. The area of modern Iraq north of Tikrīt was known in Muslim times as Al-Jazīrah, which means “the Island” and refers to the “island” between the Tigris and Euphrates rivers (i.e., Mesopotamia). To the south and west lay the Arabian Desert, inhabited largely by Arab tribesmen who occasionally acknowledged the overlordship of the Persian Sāsānian kings. Until 602 the desert frontier had been guarded by the Lakhmid kings of Al-Ḥīra, who were themselves Arabs but ruled a settled buffer state. In that year Khosrow II (Parvīz) rashly abolished the Lakhmid kingdom and laid the frontier open to nomad incursions. Farther north the western quarter was bounded by the Byzantine Empire. The frontier more or less followed the modern Syria-Iraq border and continued northward into modern Turkey, leaving Nisibis (modern Nusaybin) as the Sāsānian frontier fortress while the Byzantines held Dārā and nearby Amida (modern Diyarbakır).

IRAQ FROM C. 600 TO 1055

In 600 Iraq was a province of the Sāsānian empire, to which it had belonged for three centuries. It was probably the most populous and wealthy area in the Middle East, and the intensive irrigation agriculture of the lower Tigris and Euphrates rivers and of tributary streams such as the Diyālā and Kārūn formed the main resource base of the Sāsānian monarchy. The name Iraq was not used at this time: in the mid-6th century, the Sāsānian empire had been divided by Khosrow I into four quarters, of which the western one, called Khvarvaran, included most of modern Iraq.

The inhabitants were of mixed background. There was an aristocratic and administrative Persian upper class, but most of the population were Aramaic-speaking peasants. A considerable number of Arabs lived in the region, most of them as pastoralists along the western margins of the settled lands but some as townspeople, especially in Al-Ḥīra. In addition, there were Kurds, who lived along the foothills of the Zagros Mountains, and a large number of Greeks, mostly prisoners captured during the numerous Sāsānian campaigns into Byzantine Syria.

Ethnic diversity was matched by religious pluralism. The Sāsānian state religion, Zoroastrianism, was largely confined to the Persian ruling class. The majority of the people, especially in the northern part of the country, were probably Christians. They were sharply divided by doctrinal differences into Monophysites, linked to the Jacobite church of Syria, and Nestorians. The Nestorians were the most widespread and were tolerated by the Sāsānian kings because of their opposition to the Christians of the Roman Empire, who regarded the Nestorians as heretics. The Monophysites were regarded with more suspicion and were occasionally persecuted, but both groups were able to maintain an ecclesiastical hierarchy, and the Nestorians had an important intellectual centre at Nisibis. By that time the area around the ancient city of Babylon had a large population of Jews, both descendants of the exiles of Old Testament times and local converts. In addition, in the southern half of the country, there were numerous adherents of the old Babylonian paganism, as well as Mandaeans and Gnostics.

In the early 7th century, the stability and prosperity of this multicultural society were threatened by invasion. In 602 Khosrow II launched the last great Persian invasion of the Byzantine Empire. At first he was spectacularly successful. Syria and Egypt fell, and Constantinople (modern

Istanbul) itself was threatened. Later the tide began to turn, and in 627–628 the Byzantines, under the leadership of the emperor Heraclius, invaded Iraq and sacked the imperial capital at Ctesiphon. The invaders did not remain,

Emperor Heraclius led the Byzantine invasion of Iraq, during which the Byzantines pillaged the Sāsānian capital at Ctesiphon. Time & Life Pictures/ Getty Images

but Khosrow was discredited, deposed, and executed. There followed a period of infighting among generals and members of the royal family that left the country without clear leadership. The chaos had also damaged irrigation systems, and it was probably at this time that large areas in the south of the country reverted to marshlands, most of which remained until modern times. It was with this devastated land that the earliest Muslim raiders came into contact.

The Arab Conquest and the Early Islamic Period

The first conflict between local Bedouin tribes and Sāsānian forces seems to have been in 634, when the Arabs were defeated at the Battle of the Bridge. There a force of some 5,000 Muslims under Abū ʿUbayd al-Thaqafī was routed by the Persians. In 637 a much larger Muslim force under Saʿd ibn Abī Waqqāṣ defeated the main Persian army at the Battle of Al-Qādisiyyah and moved on to sack Ctesiphon. By the end of the following year (638), the Muslims had conquered almost all of Iraq, and the last Sāsānian king, Yazdegerd III, had fled to Iran, where he was killed in 651.

The Muslim conquest was followed by mass immigration of Arabs from eastern Arabia and Oman. These new arrivals did not disperse and settle throughout the country. Instead they established two new garrison cities, at Al-Kūfah, near ancient Babylon, and at Al-Baṣrah (Basra) in the south. The intention was that the Muslims should be a separate community of fighting men and their families living off taxes paid by the local inhabitants. In the north of the country, Mosul began to emerge as the most important city and the base of a Muslim governor and garrison. Apart from the Persian elite and the Zoroastrian priests, whose property was confiscated, most of the local people were allowed to keep their possessions and their religion.

Iraq now became a province of the Muslim caliphate, which stretched from North Africa and later Spain in the west to Sind (now southern Pakistan) in the east. At first the capital of the caliphate was at Medina, but, after the murder of the third caliph, ʿUthmān ibn ʿAffān, in 656, his successor, the Prophet Muḥammad's cousin and son-in-law ʿAlī, made Iraq his base. In 661, however, ʿAlī was murdered in Al-Kūfah, and the caliphate passed to the rival Umayyad family in Syria. Iraq became a subordinate province, even though it was the wealthiest area of the Muslim world and the one with the largest Muslim population. This situation gave rise to continual discontent with Umayyad rule that took various forms.

In 680 ʿAlī's son al-Ḥusayn arrived in Iraq from Medina, hoping that the people of Al-Kūfah would support him. They failed to act, and his small group of followers was massacred at the Battle of Karbalāʾ, but his memory lingered on as a source of inspiration for all who opposed the Umayyads. In later centuries the city of Karbalāʾ and ʿAlī's tomb at nearby Al-Najaf became important centres of Shīʿite pilgrimage that are still greatly revered today. The Iraqis had their opportunity after the death in 683 of the caliph Yazīd I when the Umayyads faced threats from many quarters. In Al-Kūfah the initiative was taken by al-Mukhtār ibn Abī ʿUbayd, who was supported by many *mawālī* (singular, *mawlā*; non-Arab converts to Islam), who felt they were treated as second-class citizens. Al-Mukhtār was killed in 687, but the Umayyads realized that strict rule was required. The caliph ʿAbd al-Malik (ruled 685–705) appointed the fearsome al-Ḥajjāj ibn Yūsuf al-Thaqafī as his governor in Iraq and all of the east. Al-Ḥajjāj became legendary as a stern but just ruler. His firm measures aroused the opposition of the local Arab elite, and in 701 there was a massive rebellion led by Muḥammad ibn al-Ash'ath. The insurrection was defeated only with the aid of Syrian soldiers. Iraq was now very much a conquered province, and al-Ḥajjāj established a new city at Wāṣit ("Medial"), halfway between Al-Kūfah and Al-Baṣrah, to be a base for a permanent Syrian garrison. In a more positive way, he encouraged Iraqis to join the expeditions led by Qutaybah ibn Muslim that between 705 and 715 conquered Central Asia for Islam. Even after al-Ḥajjāj's death in 714, the Umayyad-Syrian grip on Iraq remained firm, and resentment was widespread.

Battle of Karbalā'

The Battle of Karbalā' (Oct. 10, 680 [10th of Muharram, ah 61]) was a brief military engagement in which a small party led by al-Ḥusayn ibn 'Alī, grandson of the Prophet Muḥammad and son of 'Alī, the fourth caliph, was defeated and massacred by an army sent by the Umayyad caliph Yazīd I. The battle helped secure the position of the Umayyad dynasty, but among Shī'ite Muslims (followers of al-Ḥusayn) the 10th of Muharram (or 'Āshūrā') became an annual holy day of public mourning.

When Yazīd I succeeded his father, Mu'āwiyah I, to the caliphate in the spring of 680, the many partisans of Muḥammad's late cousin and son-in-law 'Alī ibn Abī Ṭālib—who collectively felt that leadership of the Muslim community rightly belonged to the descendants of 'Alī—rose in the city of Al-Kūfah, in what is now Iraq, and invited al-Ḥusayn to take refuge with them, promising to have him proclaimed caliph there. Meanwhile, Yazīd, having learned of the rebellious attitude of the Shī'ites in Al-Kūfah, sent 'Ubayd Allāh, governor of Al-Baṣrah, to restore order. The latter did so, summoning the chiefs of the tribes, making them responsible for the conduct of their people, and threatening reprisal. Al-Ḥusayn nevertheless set out from Mecca with all his family and retainers, expecting to be received with enthusiasm by the citizens of Al-Kūfah. However, on his arrival at Karbalā', west of the Euphrates River, on October 10, he was confronted by a large army of perhaps 4,000 men sent by 'Ubayd Allāh and under the command of 'Umar ibn Sa'd, son of the founder of Al-Kūfah. Al-Ḥusayn, whose retinue mustered only 72 fighting men, gave battle, vainly relying on the promised aid from Al-Kūfah, and fell with almost all his family and followers. The bodies of the dead, including that of al-Ḥusayn, were then mutilated, only adding to the consternation of later generations of Shī'ites.

Though it was a rash expedition, it did involve the grandson of the Prophet and thus many members of the Prophet's family. Al-Ḥusayn's devout partisans at Al-Kūfah, who by their overtures had been the principal cause of the disaster, regarded it as a tragedy, and the facts gradually acquired a romantic and spiritual colouring. 'Umar, 'Ubayd Allāh, and even Yazīd came to be regarded by 'Alī's supporters as murderers, and their names have ever since been held accursed by Shī'ite Muslims. Shī'ites observe the 10th of Muharram as a day of public mourning; and, among Iranians especially, as well as in Karbalā', passion plays (Arabic *ta'ziyyah*) are enacted, representing the misfortunes of the family of 'Alī. The tomb of the decapitated martyr al-Ḥusayn at Karbalā' is their most holy place.

The 'Abbāsid Caliphate

Opposition to the Umayyads finally came to a head in northeastern Iran (Khorāsān) in 747 when the *mawlā* Abū Muslim raised black banners in the name of the 'Abbāsids, a branch of the family of the Prophet, distantly related to 'Alī and his descendants. In 749 the armies from the east reached Iraq, where they received the support of much of the population. The 'Abbāsids themselves came from their secluded estate at Ḥumaymah in southern Jordan, and in 749 the first 'Abbāsid caliph, Abū al-'Abbās (al-Saffāḥ), was proclaimed in the mosque at Al-Kūfah. This "'Abbāsid Revolution" ushered in the golden age of Islamic Iraq. Khorāsān was too much on the fringes of the Muslim world to be a suitable capital, and from the beginning the ʿAbbāsid caliphs made Iraq their base. By this time Islam in Iraq had spread well beyond the original garrison towns, even though Muslims were still a minority of the population.

At first the ʿAbbāsids ruled from Al-Kūfah or nearby, but in 762 al-Manṣūr (ruled 754–775) founded a new capital on the site of the old village of Baghdad. It was officially known as Madīnat al-Salām ("City of Peace"), but in popular usage the old name prevailed. Baghdad soon became larger than any other city in either Europe or the Middle East. Al-Manṣūr built the massive Round City with four gates and his palace and the main mosque in the centre. This Round City was exclusively a government quarter, and soon after its construction the markets were banished to the Karkh suburb to the south. Other suburbs soon grew up, developed by leading courtiers: Ḥarbiyyah to the northeast, where the Khorāsānī soldiers were settled, and, across the Tigris on the east bank, a new palace quarter for the caliph's son and heir al-Mahdī (ruled 775–785). The siting of Baghdad proved to be an act of genius. It had access to both the Tigris and the Euphrates river systems and was close to the main route through the Zagros Mountains to the Iranian plateau. Wheat and barley from Al-Jazīrah and dates and rice from Al-Baṣrah and the south could be transported in by water. By the year 800 the city may have had as many as 500,000 inhabitants and was an important commercial centre as well as the seat of government. The city grew at the expense of other centres, and both the old Sāsānian capital at Ctesiphon (called Al-Madāʾin, "the Cities," by the Arabs) and the early Islamic centre at Al-Kūfah fell into decline.

The high point of prosperity was probably reached in the reign of Hārūn al-Rashīd (ruled 786–809), when Iraq was very much the centre of the empire and riches flowed into the capital from throughout the Muslim world. The prosperity and order in the southern part of the country were, however, offset by outbreaks of lawlessness in Al-Jazīrah, notably the rebellion of the Bedouin Walīd ibn Ṭarīf, who defied government forces between 794 and 797. Even the most powerful governments found it difficult to extend their authority beyond the limits of the settled land.

Much more serious disruption followed the death of Hārūn in 809. He left his son al-Amīn (ruled 809–813) as caliph in Baghdad but divided the caliphate and gave his son al-Ma'mūn (ruled 813–833) control over Iran and the eastern half of the empire. This arrangement soon broke down, and there ensued a prolonged and devastating civil war. The supporters of al-Amīn made an ill-judged attempt to invade Iran in the spring of 811 and were soundly defeated at Rayy (just south of Tehran in modern Iran). Al-Ma'mūn's supporters retaliated by invading Iraq, and, from August 812 until September 813, they laid siege to Baghdad while the rest of Iraq slid into anarchy. The collapse of Baghdadi resistance and the death of al-Amīn did not improve matters, for al-Ma'mūn, now generally recognized as caliph, decided to rule from Merv in distant Khorāsān (near modern Mary, in Turkmenistan). This downgrading of Iraq united many different groups in prolonged and bitter resistance to al-Ma'mūn's governor and led to another siege of Baghdad. Finally, al-Ma'mūn was forced to concede that he could not rule from a distance, and in August 819 he returned to Baghdad.

Once again Iraq was the central province of the caliphate and Baghdad the capital, but the prolonged conflict had left much of the city in ruins and caused great destruction in the countryside. It probably marked the beginning of a long decline in the prosperity of the area that became pronounced from the 9th century onward.

Al-Ma'mūn sent his generals, including the highly effective Ṭāhir al-Ḥusayn, to bring Syria and Egypt back under 'Abbāsid rule and set about restoring the government apparatus, many of the administrative records having been destroyed in the fighting. During al-Ma'mūn's reign in Baghdad (819–833), Iraq became the centre of remarkable cultural activity, notably translations of Greek science and philosophy into Arabic. The caliph himself collected texts, employed such translators as the celebrated Ḥunayn ibn Isḥāq, and established an academy in Baghdad, the Bayt al-Ḥikmah ("House of Wisdom"), with a library and an observatory. Private patrons such as the Banū Mūsā brothers followed his example. This activity had a profound effect not only on Muslim intellectual life but also on the intellectual life of western Europe, for much of the science and philosophy taught in universities in the Middle Ages was derived from these Arabic translations, rendered into Latin in Spain in the 12th century. Under al-Ma'mūn the Mu'tazilite creed (a school of theology greatly indebted to Hellenistic rationalism) was declared state dogma—one of the few instances of such an act in Islamic history—and was not abandoned until the caliphate of al-Mutawakkil some 20 years later.

Politically, the position was less rosy. Although Al-Ma'mūn regained control of much territory lost by the caliphate, he granted virtual autonomy to military governors, or emirs, such as Ṭāhir. This practice spiraled out of control under later caliphs, and eastern dynasties such as the Ṭāhirids and Sāmānids were the first of many independent entities to arise within the caliphal realm. Al-Ma'mūn was also unable to recruit sufficient forces to replace the old 'Abbāsid army that had been destroyed in the civil war, and he became increasingly dependent on his younger brother, Abū Isḥāq, who had gathered a small but highly efficient force of Turkish mercenaries, many of them slaves or former slaves from Central Asia. When al-Ma'mūn died in 833, Abū Isḥāq, under the title al-Mu'taṣim (ruled 833–842), succeeded him without difficulty. Al-Mu'taṣim was no intellectual but rather an effective soldier and administrator. His reign marks the introduction into Iraq of an alien, usually Turkish, military class, which was to dominate the political life of the country, and much of the region, for centuries to come. From that time Iraqi Arabs were rarely employed in military positions, though they continued to be influential in the civil administration.

The recruitment of this new military class provoked resentment among the Baghdadis, who felt that they were being excluded from power. This resentment led al-Mu'taṣim to found a new capital at Sāmarrā', the last major urban foundation in Iraq until the 20th century. He chose a site on the Tigris about 100 miles (160 km) north of Baghdad. There he laid out a city with palaces and mosques, broad straight streets, and a regular pattern of housing. The ruins of this city, which was expanded by the caliph al-Mutawwakil (ruled 847–861), can still be seen on the ground and, more strikingly, in aerial photographs, in which the whole plan can be discerned. Sāmarrā' became a vast city, but it had none of the natural advantages of Baghdad: communication by river and canal with the Euphrates and southern Iraq was much more difficult, and in spite of massive investment the water supply was always inadequate. Sāmarrā' survived only while it was the capital of the caliphate, from 836 to 892. When the caliphs returned to Baghdad, it showed no independent urban vitality and soon shrank to a small provincial town—which is why its remains can still be seen when all traces of early 'Abbāsid Baghdad have disappeared.

For nearly 30 years the new regime worked well, and Iraq was for the last time the centre of a large empire. Tax revenues from other areas enriched Sāmarrā', and Baghdad

Remains in Sāmarrā' include this spiral minaret, built in the 'Abbāsid period. Oleg Nikishin/Getty Images

continued to prosper under the rule of the Ṭāhirids. Al-Baṣrah remained a great entrepôt on the Persian Gulf. The employment of Turkish soldiers without any ties to the local community gave rise to political instability, however. In 861 al-Mutawwakil was assassinated in his palace in Sāmarrā' by disaffected troops, and there began a nine-year anarchy in which the Turkish soldiers made and deposed caliphs virtually at will. The office of the caliph's senior military officer, the *amīr al-umarā'*, became the most powerful position in Baghdad. In 865 open civil war raged between Sāmarrā' and Baghdad and resulted in another destructive siege of Baghdad.

The anarchy played itself out, and in 870 stability was restored with the caliph al-Mu'tamid in Sāmarrā' as titular ruler and his dynamic military brother al-Muwaffaq exercising real power in Baghdad, but the anarchy had done real and lasting damage to Iraq. Almost all the provinces of the empire, both the Iranian lands in the east (where the Ṣaffārids joined the Ṭāhirids and Sāmānids as an independent dynasty) and Syria and Egypt (where the Ṭūlūnids gained autonomy) to the west, had broken away. Worse, a major social revolt had broken out in southern Iraq itself. In the prosperous years of early Islamic Iraq, large numbers of slaves had been imported from East Africa to be used in grueling agricultural work in the marshes of southern Iraq. In an episode known as the Zanj rebellion (869–883), the slaves rose up, led by an Arab who claimed to be a descendant of ʿAlī. This rebellion was extremely serious for the ʿAbbāsid government: it laid waste to large areas of agricultural land, and the great trading port of Al-Baṣrah was taken and sacked in 871, the rebels burning mosques and houses and massacring the inhabitants with indiscriminate ferocity. Although Al-Baṣrah was soon recaptured, it never fully recovered, and trade shifted down the gulf to cities such as Sīrāf (modern Bandar-e Ṭāherī) in southern Iran. The crushing of this revolt involved long and hard amphibious campaigns in the marshes, led by al-Muwaffaq and his son Abū al-ʿAbbās (later the caliph al-Muʿtaḍid) from 879 until the rebel stronghold at Mukhtārah was finally taken in 883.

During the reigns of al-Muʿtaḍid (ruled 892–902) and his son al-Muktafī (ruled 902–908), Iraq was united under ʿAbbāsid control. Once more Baghdad was the capital, although the caliphs had largely abandoned the Round City of al-Manṣūr on the west bank, and the centre of government now lay on the east bank in the area that has remained the centre of the city ever since. It was a period of great cultural activity, and Baghdad was home to many intellectuals, including the great historian al-Ṭabarī, whose vast work chronicled the early history of the Muslim state. However, it was no longer the capital of a great empire.

During the reign of the boy caliph al-Muqtadir (ruled 908–932), the political situation rapidly deteriorated. The weakness of the caliph gave rise to endless intrigues among parties of viziers and to a growing tendency for the military to take matters into its own hands. Increasingly the government in Baghdad lost control of the revenues and lands of Iraq. In 935 the final crisis occurred when the caliph al-Rāḍī was obliged to hand over all real secular power to an ambitious general, Ibn Rā'iq.

The political catastrophe of the 'Abbāsid Caliphate was accompanied by economic collapse. It is probable that the vicious circle of decline started with the civil war after Hārūn's death in 809, and there can be no doubt that it was exacerbated by the demands of the Turkish military for payment. Administrators increasingly resorted to short-term expedients such as tax farming (auctioning the right of taxation to the highest bidder), which encouraged extortion and oppression, and granting *iqṭā's* to the military. In theory, *iqṭā's* were grants of the right to collect and use tax revenues; they could not be inherited or sold. The purpose of an *iqṭā'* was for the soldiers themselves to collect what they could directly from lands assigned to them. Both these remedies put a premium on short-term exploitation of land rather than long-term investment. Except in the north, most Iraqi agriculture depended on investment in and upkeep of complex irrigation works, and these new fiscal systems proved disastrous. In 935, the same year in which al-Rāḍī handed over power to the military leader Ibn Rā'iq, the greatest of the ancient irrigation works of central Iraq, the Nahrawān canal, was breached to impede an advancing army. The damage was never repaired, large areas went out of cultivation, and villages were abandoned. The destruction of the canal is symbolic of the end of the irrigation culture that had brought great wealth to ancient Mesopotamia and that had underpinned Sāsānian and early Islamic government.

The Būyid Period (932–1062)

After a decade of chaos, during which Ibn Rā'iq and other military leaders struggled for power, an element of stability was regained in 945 when Baghdad was taken by the Būyid chief, Muʿizz al-Dawlah. The Būyids were leaders of the Daylamite people from the area southwest of the Caspian Sea. These hardy mountaineers had taken advantage of the prevailing anarchy to take over much of western Iran in 934, and they now moved into Iraq. Muʿizz al-Dawlah established himself in Baghdad, but his regime never ruled over all of Iraq. In the capital itself a state of tension developed between the Daylamites and the Turks, who had for many years been the main military force. Moreover, when the Būyids made known their adherence to the Shīʿite branch of Islam, there was further, often violent, tension between their supporters and the Sunnis, who were in the majority. Baghdad began to disintegrate into a number of small communities, each either Sunni or Shīʿite and each with its own walls to protect it from its neighbours. Large areas, including much of the Round City of al-Manṣūr, fell into ruin. Further problems were caused by the loss of control of Al-Jazīrah in the north of Iraq, for it was from this area that Baghdad had traditionally received its grain supplies. The city was too populous to be fed from its own hinterland, and, when political conflict interrupted the grain supplies from Al-Jazīrah, famine was added to the other miseries of the people. In one area, however, the Būyids retained the old forms: rather than make a clean break, they allowed the ʿAbbāsid caliphs to remain in comfortable but secluded captivity in their palace in Baghdad.

Those who forgot where real power lay, however, were soon brutally reminded.

From the beginning of the 10th century, Iraq was usually divided politically, and the Būyids in Baghdad seldom controlled the whole area as their 'Abbāsid predecessors had done. The area around Al-Baṣrah in the south was frequently in the hands of rival Būyid princes, and the north increasingly went its own way.

The economic decline and the ruin of irrigation systems that had affected central and southern Iraq do not seem to have been as marked in Al-Jazīrah, where agriculture was largely dry farming, dependent on precipitation levels. The area was consequently less potentially wealthy than the south but also less vulnerable to political upset. Mosul had been the most important city in Al-Jazīrah since the Islamic conquest, and it now became an important regional capital. The area was dominated by the Ḥamdānid dynasty (905/6–1004). Originally, leaders of the Taghlib Bedouin tribe of Al-Jazīrah, members of this family had taken service in the 'Abbāsid armies. In 935 their leader, Nāṣir al-Dawlah, was acknowledged as ruler of Mosul in exchange for a money tribute and the provision of grain for Baghdad and Sāmarrā', however, neither money nor grain was paid on a regular basis. The Ḥamdānids strengthened their position by recruiting Turkish soldiers for their army and by establishing good relations with the leaders of the Kurdish tribes in the hills to the north.

In 967 Nāṣir al-Dawlah was succeeded by his son Abū Taghlib, but in 977 the greatest of the Būyids of Iraq, 'Aḍud al-Dawlah, took Mosul and drove the Ḥamdānids out. This triumph did not unite Iraq for long. After 'Aḍud al-Dawlah died in 983, his more feeble successors allowed northern Iraq to slip from their hands. Increasingly, power in the north was assumed by the sheikhs of the Banū 'Uqayl, the largest Bedouin tribe in Al-Jazīrah. By the early

11th century, the leader of the ʿUqaylid dynasty (ruled *c.* 990-1169), Qirwāsh ibn al-Muqallad, dominated Mosul and Al-Jazīrah. Unlike the Ḥamdānids and the Būyids, the ʿUqaylid sheikhs lived in desert encampments rather than in cities, and they relied on their tribesmen rather than on Turkish or Daylamite soldiers. By 1010 Qirwāsh's power extended as far south as Al-Kūfah, though Baghdad itself never came under Bedouin control, and he tried to arrange an alliance with the caliphs of the Fāṭimid dynasty of Egypt. From then on his power declined, and in the early 1040s the Banū ʿUqayl found themselves threatened by a new enemy, the Oghuz Turkish tribes invading from Iran. In 1044, northwest of Mosul, these Turks and the Bedouin Arabs fought a major battle, in which the Turks were soundly defeated. Although little reported by historians, it is probable that this battle ensured that the people of the plains of northern Iraq remained Arabic-speaking, unlike the inhabitants of the steppelands of Anatolia to the north, who thereafter spoke Turkish.

In the south, too, the Bedouin became increasingly powerful. On the desert frontier in the Al-Kūfah area, the Banū Mazyad, the leading sheikhs of the Asad tribe, established a small state that reached its apogee during the long reign of Dubays I (1018–1081). During that time the main camp (Arabic: *ḥillah*) of the Mazyadid dynasty (ruled 961–1150) became an important town and, under the name Al-Ḥillah, replaced early Islamic Al-Kūfah as the largest urban centre in the area.

Baghdad and the surrounding area from the lower Tigris south to the Persian Gulf remained more or less under Būyid rule. In 978 Baghdad was taken by the Būyid ruler of Fārs (southwestern Iran), ʿAḍud al-Dawlah. In the five years before his death in 983, he made a serious attempt to rebuild the administration, to control the Bedouin, and to reunite Mosul with southern Iraq. In addition to being a patron of learning, he made efforts to restore damaged irrigation systems. Such determination, however, was rare, and after his death his lands were divided. The later Būyids had great difficulty in governing even Baghdad and the immediately surrounding area. Poverty compounded their problems. Jalāl al-Dawlah (ruled 1025–1044) was obliged to send away his servants and release his horses because he could no longer afford to feed them.

Baghdad presented a picture of devastation in this period. Brigands maintained themselves by kidnapping and extortion, and disputes between the Sunnis and the Shīʿites became increasingly violent. Although less numerous, the Shīʿites were sometimes encouraged by Būyid princes who wished to win their support. This prompted the Sunnis to look to the ʿAbbāsid caliphs for leadership. The caliph al-Qādir (ruled 991–1031) assumed the religious leadership of the Sunnis and published a manifesto, the *Risālat al-Qādiriyyah* (1029), in which the main tenets of Sunni belief were outlined. He did not, however, attain any significant political power. In spite of this disorder and political chaos, Baghdad remained an intellectual centre. The lack of firm political authority meant that free debate and exchange of ideas could take place in a way that was not possible under more authoritarian regimes.

This anarchic but culturally productive era in the history of Iraq came to an end in December 1055 when the Seljuq Turkish leader Toghrıl Beg entered the city with his forces and rapidly established a secure government over most of Iraq. The country had seen many changes since the 7th century. Much of the ethnic and religious diversity of late Sāsānian Iraq had disappeared. Apart from the Turkish military and the Kurds of the mountainous areas, most people now spoke one dialect or another of Arabic. There were still Christian communities, especially in the northern areas around Tikrīt and Mosul, but the majority of the population was now Muslim. Within the Muslim community, however, there were serious divisions between Sunnis and Shīʿites. Iraq had also lost its position as the wealthiest area of the Middle East. There are no census figures, but it is reasonable to assume that the population had declined significantly, and it is clear that many able and enterprising people sought to escape the chaos by migrating to Egypt. Iraq had lost its imperial role forever.

IRAQ FROM 1055 TO 1534

During the subsequent five centuries, the name Iraq (ʿIrāq) referred to two distinct geopolitical regions. The first, qualified as Arabian Iraq (*ʿIrāq ʿArabī*), denoted the area roughly corresponding to ancient Mesopotamia or the modern nation of Iraq and consisted of Upper Iraq or Al-Jazīrah and Lower Iraq or Al-Sawād ("The Black [Lands]"). The town of Tikrīt was traditionally considered to mark the border between these two entities. The second region, lying to the east of Arabian Iraq and separated from it by the Zagros Mountains, was called foreign (i.e., Persian) Iraq (*ʿIrāq ʿAjamī*) and was more or less identical with ancient Media or the Umayyad and ʿAbbāsid province of Jibāl. Together these regions became known as "the Two Iraqs," in contradistinction to the previous usage of the term in reference to the towns of Al-Baṣrah and Al-Kūfah, the two major urban settlements of Lower Iraq in early Islamic times.

In addition, Arabian Iraq was subdivided into three political spheres: Upper Iraq, centred on the town of Mosul; Middle Iraq, or the area around Baghdad; and Lower Iraq, whose major centres were the towns of Al-Ḥillah, Wāṣit, and Al-Baṣrah. Upper Iraq had strong political ties to the provinces of Diyār Bakr and Diyār Rabīʿah in eastern Anatolia (now part of Turkey) and northern Syria as well as with Azerbaijan. Middle and Lower

Iraq were bound politically both to Azerbaijan and to Persian Iraq. Traditionally, all three spheres were subject to pressures from the greater powers of the Iranian plateau and the Nile valley.

On the eve of the Turkish Seljuq invasion of the central Islamic lands, these spheres were dominated by three different groups. Upper Iraq was in the hands of the ʿUqaylids, a Shīʿite Arab dynasty of Bedouin origin. In Middle Iraq the Shīʿite Daylamite Būyid generalissimos had controlled both the city of Baghdad and the person of the caliph since the first half of the 10th century. Lower Iraq was held by another Shīʿite Bedouin Arab dynasty, the Mazyadids. Both the ʿUqaylids and the Mazyadids had initially gained their power bases (in Mosul and Al-Ḥillah, respectively) as dependents of the Būyids. Moreover, both had supported the Būyids in resisting the Seljuq invaders.

The Seljuqs (1055–1152)

The Sunni Seljuq leader Toghrıl Beg entered Baghdad in December 1055, arresting and imprisoning the Būyid prince al-Malik al-Raḥīm. Without meeting the ʿAbbāsid caliph, he proceeded against the ʿUqaylids in Mosul, taking the city in 1057 and retaining the ʿUqaylid ruler as governor there on behalf of the Seljuqs. On his return to Baghdad in 1058, Toghrıl was finally received by the caliph al-Qāʾim (ruled 1031–75), who granted him the title "king of the East and West."

In 1058, with Toghrıl busy elsewhere, the Būyid slave general Arslān al-Muẓaffar al-Basāsīrī and the ʿUqaylid ruler Quraysh ibn Badrān (ruled 1052–61) occupied Baghdad, recognizing al-Mustanṣir, the Shīʿite Fāṭimid caliph of Egypt and Syria, and sending him the insignia of rule as trophies. Al-Basāsīrī expelled al-Qāʾim and, with the help of the Mazyadid Dubays, quickly extended his control over Wāṣit and Al-Baṣrah. Both the Fāṭimids and the Mazyadids withdrew their support, however, and al-Basāsīrī was killed by Seljuq forces in 1060. Toghrıl reinstated al-Qā'im as caliph, who then gave him additional honours, including the title sultan (Arabic: *sulṭān*, "authority"), found on coins minted in the names of both the caliph and the sultan. The Seljuqs now tried to rid Iraq of all Shīʿite influences.

Exchanging Shīʿite Būyid emirs for Sunni Seljuq sultans, while perhaps ideologically appropriate, made little practical difference for the ʿAbbāsid caliphs, who remained captives in the hands of military strongmen. Though Baghdad continued as the seat of the caliphate, the Seljuq sultans ultimately established their capital at Eṣfahān in Persian Iraq. The relations between caliph and sultan were formalized by the great theologian al-Ghazālī (d. 1111):

> *Government in these days is a consequence solely of military power, and whosoever he may be to whom the holder of military power gives his allegiance, that person is Caliph. And whosoever exercises independent authority, so long as he shows allegiance to the Caliph in the matter of his prerogatives [of sovereignty], the same is a sultan, whose commands and judgments are valid in the several parts of the earth.*

These and other politico-religious doctrines were universalized through the spread of a system of educational institutions (madrasahs), associated with the powerful Seljuq minister Niẓām al-Mulk (d. 1092), an Iranian from Khorāsān. The institutions were called Niẓāmiyyahs in his honour. The best known of them, the Baghdad Niẓāmiyyah, was founded in 1067. Niẓām al-Mulk argued for the creation of a strong central political authority, focused on the sultan and modeled on the polities of the pre-Islamic Sāsānians of Iran and of certain early Islamic rulers. Under the successors of Toghrıl, especially Alp-Arslan (ruled 1063–72) and Malik-Shah (ruled 1072–92), the so-called Great Seljuq empire did attain a certain degree of centralization, and the sultans and princes went on to conquer eastern and central Anatolia in the name of Islam and to eject the Shīʿite Fāṭimids from Syria.

In the second half of the 11th and the first half of the 12th centuries, the Seljuq Turks gradually established more or less direct rule over all of Arabian Iraq. In 1096 the ʿUqaylids of Upper Iraq were finally overthrown by the Syrian branch of the Seljuq family. Upper Iraq now came under the rule of Seljuq princes and their governors, who were often of servile origin. One of these governors, ʿImād al-Dīn Zangī, with the decline of the power of his Seljuq masters, founded an independent dynasty, the Zangids, and a branch of this dynasty ruled Mosul from 1127 to 1222. At the time of the Mongol invasions, Mosul was in the hands of the slave general Badr al-Dīn Luʾluʾ (ruled 1222–59). In Lower Iraq the Mazyadids were able to extend their influence, taking the towns of Hīt, Wāṣit, Al-Baṣrah, and Tikrīt in the early 1100s. In 1108, however, their king, Ṣadaqah, was defeated and killed by the Seljuq sultan Muḥammad Tapar (ruled 1105–18), and the dynasty never regained its former importance. The Mazyadids were finally dispossessed by the Seljuqs in the second half of the 12th century, and their capital, Al-Ḥillah, was occupied by caliphal forces.

The Later ʿAbbāsids (1152–1258)

With the death of Muḥammad Tapar, the Great Seljuq state was in effect partitioned between Muḥammad's brother Sanjar (ruled 1096/97–1157), headquartered at Merv in Khorāsān, and his son Maḥmūd II (ruled 1118–31), centred on Hamadān in Persian Iraq. These Iraq Seljuq sultans unsuccessfully tried to maintain their control over the 'Abbāsid caliph in Baghdad. In 1135 the caliph al-Mustarshid (ruled 1118–35) personally led an army against the sultan Mas'ūd, but he was defeated and later assassinated. Al-Mustarshid's brother, al-Muqtafī (ruled 1136–60), was appointed by Sultan Mas'ūd to succeed him as caliph. After Mas'ūd's death al-Muqtafī was able to establish a caliphal state based on Baghdad by conquering Al-Ḥillah, Al-Kūfah, Wāṣit, and Tikrīt.

By far the most important figure in the revival of independent caliphal authority in Arabian Iraq and the surrounding area—after more than 200 years of secular military domination, first under the Būyids and then the Seljuqs—was the caliph al-Nāṣir (ruled 1180–1225). For nearly half a century, he tried to rally the Islamic world under the banner of 'Abbāsid universalism, not only politically, by emphasizing the necessity for the support of caliphal causes, but also morally, by attempting to reconcile the Sunnis and the Shī'ites. In addition, he tried to gain control of various voluntary associations such as the mystico-religious (Sufi) brotherhoods and the craft-associated youth (*futuwwah*) organizations. He also began the dangerous precedent of allying himself with powers in Khorāsān and Central Asia against the traditional caliphal adversaries in Persian Iraq. Through this policy he was able to rid himself of the last Iraq Seljuq sultan, Toghrıl III (ruled 1176–94), who was killed by the Khwārezm-Shah 'Alā' al-Din Tekish (ruled 1172–1200), the ruler of the province lying along the lower course of the Amu Darya (ancient Oxus River) in Central Asia. When Tekish insisted on greater formal recognition from the caliph a few years later, al-Nāṣir refused, and inconclusive fighting broke out between the two. The conflict came to a head under Tekish's son, the Khwārezm-Shah 'Alā' al-Dīn Muḥammad (ruled 1200–20), who demanded that the caliph renounce the temporal power built up by the later 'Abbāsids after the decline of the Iraq Seljuqs. When negotiations broke down, Muḥammad declared al-Nāṣir deposed, proclaimed an eastern Iranian notable as anticaliph, and marched on Baghdad. In 1217 Muḥammad seized most of western Iran, but, just as he was about to fall on al-Nāṣir's capital, his army was decimated by a blizzard in the Zagros Mountains. These events afforded al-Nāṣir and his successors only a brief respite from dangers arising in the east.

The Mongol Il-Khans (1258–1335)

At the time of al-Nāṣir's death in 1225, the Mongols under Genghis Khan had already destroyed the state of the Khwārezm-Shahs and conquered much of northern Iran. The armies of the 'Abbāsid caliph al-Mustanṣir (ruled 1226–42), al-Nāṣir's grandson, managed to drive off a Mongol attack on Arabian Iraq. Under his son, al-Musta'ṣim, Baghdad resisted a siege by the Mongols in 1245. A series of terrible floods in 1243, 1253, 1255, and 1256 undermined the defenses of the city, the prosperity of the region, and the confidence of the populace. In 1258 Baghdad was surrounded by a major Mongol force commanded by the non-Muslim Hülegü, a grandson of Genghis Khan, who had been sent from Mongolia expressly to deal with the 'Abbāsids. The city fell on Feb. 10, 1258, and al-Musta'ṣim was executed shortly thereafter. Although the Mamlūk sultans of Egypt and Syria later raised a figurehead, or "shadow," caliph in Cairo, and after the Ottoman conquest

Hülegü, a grandson of Genghis Khan, leading the assault on Baghdad, 1258.
Bildarchiv Preussischer Kulturbesitz/Art Resource, NY

of Egypt in 1517 the Ottoman sultans used the title caliph until the Ottoman "caliphate" was abolished by Mustafa Kemal (Atatürk) in 1924, the death of al-Musta'ṣim—the last universally recognized caliph—in fact represents the end of this great Islamic religio-political institution. Physically much of Baghdad was destroyed, and it is said that 800,000 of its inhabitants perished. Administratively, the city was relegated to the status of a provincial centre. Other cities in Arabian Iraq, such as Al-Ḥillah, Al-Kūfah, and Al-Baṣrah, readily came to terms with the conqueror and were spared. In Upper Iraq, Mosul was made the capital of the provinces of Diyār Bakr and Diyār Rabīʿah. These provinces, like Arabian Iraq, were dependencies of the new Il-Khan Mongol polity, which was based in Azerbaijan. (The Il-Khans in turn were nominally subordinate to the Great Khan in China.) Although Baghdad may have retained a certain symbolic aura for Muslims, the city of Tabrīz in Azerbaijan rapidly replaced it as the major commercial and political hub of the region.

Mongol rule in Baghdad and Mosul generally took the form of a condominium consisting of a Muslim, Christian, or Jewish civilian administrator seconded by a Mongol garrison commander. Although under the Muslim Juvaynī family of Khorāsān (ruled 1258–85) there is some evidence that Baghdad began to recover somewhat from the devastation it had suffered at the hands of the Mongols, in general Iraq experienced a period of severe political and economic decline that was to last well into the 16th century. Later on, in spite of the conversion to Islam of the Il-Khan Maḥmūd Ghāzān (ruled 1295–1304) and the centralizing reforms of his minister Rashīd al-Dīn (d. 1318), according to one source, by 1335–40 state or *dīwān* revenues in Arabian Iraq had fallen to one-tenth of their pre-Mongol level.

Il-Khanid Successors (1335–1410)

With the death of the last effective Il-Khan, Abū Saʿīd Bahādur Khan in 1335, intense rivalry broke out among the chieftains of the Mongol military elite, especially the leaders of the Süldüz and Jalāyirid tribes. The Süldüz, also known as the Chūpānids, made Azerbaijan their stronghold, while the Jalāyirid took control in Baghdad. At first both groups raised a succession of Il-Khanid figureheads to legitimize their rule.

The most prominent of the Jalāyirids, Sheikh Uways (ruled 1356–74), finally wrested control of Azerbaijan from the Süldüz Chūpānids in 1360, creating a polity based on Arabian Iraq and Azerbaijan. In addition to engaging in this and other military exploits, he fostered trade and commerce and won renown as a patron of poetry, painting, and calligraphy. He also undertook a number of architectural projects in Baghdad.

The later Jalāyirids, however, dissipated their energies in fruitless foreign adventures and fratricidal struggles. In 1393, during the reign of Sultan Aḥmad Jalāyir, Timur (Tamerlane), a new conqueror from Central Asia, took Baghdad and Tikrīt. Aḥmad was able to reoccupy his capital briefly, but Timur again besieged and sacked Baghdad in 1401, dealing it a blow from which it did not recover until modern times. Timurid administration in Arabian Iraq, first under Timur and later under his grandson Abū Bakr, was sporadic and short-lived: they controlled the area during the years 1393–94, 1401–02, and 1403–05. After Timur's death Aḥmad regained Baghdad for a time, but in 1410 he was killed in a dispute with his former ally Kara Yūsuf, chief of the Kara Koyunlu ("Black Sheep") Turkmen tribal confederation from eastern Anatolia, who had just driven the Timurids out of Azerbaijan. The remnants of the Jalāyirid dynasty were pushed south to Al-Ḥillah, Wāṣit, and Al-Baṣrah. They were finally extinguished by the Kara Koyunlu in 1432.

THE TURKMEN (1410–1508)

In the 15th century two Turkmen tribal confederations vied for control of Iraq. The first of these was the Kara Koyunlu, which since about 1375 had ruled the area from Mosul to Erzurum in eastern Anatolia as supporters of the Jalāyirids. After seizing Arabian Iraq, Kara Yūsuf turned the province over to his son Shah Muḥammad, who held Baghdad until 1433. He in turn was dispossessed by his brother Ispān (or Eṣfahān) until yet another of Kara Yūsuf's sons, Jahān Shah (ruled 1438–67), took the city. He, his sons, and their deputies held Baghdad from 1447 to 1468, when they were ousted by their archrivals, the Ak Koyunlu ("White Sheep") Turkmen confederation, led by Uzun Ḥasan (ruled 1457–78). Like the Kara Koyunlu, the Ak Koyunlu came from eastern Anatolia.

Although significant achievements in the arts are recorded from the first half of the 15th century, scholars generally reckon this period one of the darkest in the history of the area. Ak Koyunlu rule in Baghdad (1468–1508) for the most part appears to have been somewhat less turbulent than that of the Kara Koyunlu, though later the Pūrnāk tribe—whose chieftains controlled the city intermittently from 1475 to 1508—were pitted against the Mawṣillū tribe in Upper Iraq. After the partitioning of the Ak Koyunlu state in 1500, Arabian Iraq became the final foothold of the last Turkmen ruler, Murād (ruled 1497–1508, d. 1514), until the Ṣafavid conquest.

Both the Kara Koyunlu and the Ak Koyunlu governors of Baghdad were forced to deal with the messianic ultra-Shīʿite uprising of the Mushaʿshaʿ in Lower Iraq. In 1436 Muḥammad ibn Falāḥ, the founder of the Mushaʿshaʿ sect, made his appearance among the Arab tribes in the marshy regions around Wāṣit, conquered the town of Ḥawīzah (modern Hoveyzeh, Iran), and mounted an expedition

Kara Koyunlu

The Kara Koyunlu (Turkish: Karakoyunlular; English: Black Sheep) was a Turkmen tribal federation that ruled Azerbaijan and Iraq from about 1375 to 1468. The Kara Koyunlu were vassals of the Jalāyirid dynasty of Baghdad and Tabrīz from about 1375, when the head of their leading tribe, Kara Muḥammad Turmush (ruled *c.* 1375–89), ruled Mosul. The federation secured its independence with the seizure of Tabrīz, which became its capital, by Kara Yūsuf (ruled 1390–1400; 1406–20). Routed by the armies of Timur in 1400, Kara Yūsuf sought refuge with the Mamlūks of Egypt but by 1406 was able to regain Tabrīz. He then secured the Kara Koyunlu position against threats from the Ak Koyunlu ("White Sheep"), a rival Turkmen federation in the province of Diyār Bakr (modern Iraq), and from the Georgians and Shīrvān-Shahs in the Caucasus and Timur's successors in Iran. The capture of Baghdad in 1410 and the installation of a subsidiary Kara Koyunlu line there hastened the downfall of the Jalāyirids themselves.

In spite of the dynastic struggles for primacy in the years following Kara Yūsuf's death (1420) and continuing Timurid pressure, the Kara Koyunlu maintained a firm grip on their possessions. Jahān Shah (ruled *c.* 1438–67) established a temporary peace with the Timurid Shāh Rokh, who had helped him gain the Kara Koyunlu throne. After Shāh Rokh's death in 1447, however, Jahān Shah annexed portions of Iraq and the eastern coast of the Arabian Peninsula as well as Timurid western Iran. Jahān Shah's rule was repeatedly troubled, however, by his rebellious sons and by the semiautonomous Kara Koyunlu rulers of Baghdad, whom he expelled in 1464. An attempt to take Diyār Bakr from the Ak Koyunlu in 1466 ended in Jahān Shah's defeat and death, and within two years the Kara Koyunlu succumbed to the superior Ak Koyunlu forces.

against Al-Baṣrah. His son 'Alī took Wāṣit and Al-Najaf, raiding Baghdad and attacking pilgrim caravans. Toward the end of the 15th century, this movement was brought under control temporarily by the Turkmen regimes.

The Ṣafavids (1508–34)

In October 1508, Shah Ismāʿīl I, founder of the Shīʿite Ṣafavid dynasty in Iran, entered Baghdad at the head of his Kizilbash Turkmen troops, driving out the Pūrnāk governor. Turning the city over to his chief of staff, he moved south against the Mushaʿshaʿ. As in the Turkmen period, tribal centrifugalism continued to dominate the politics of the region.

In Upper Iraq parts of Diyār Bakr—including Mosul and the Kurdish regions east of the Tigris—came under Ottoman control after the Ṣafavids under Ismāʿīl were defeated by Sultan Selim I (ruled 1512–20) at the Battle of Chāldirān in 1514. Arabian Iraq, however, remained in Ṣafavid hands, and the Mawṣillū chieftains, formerly confederates of the Ak Koyunlu, now in the service of the Ṣafavids, rose to power in Baghdad between 1514 and 1529. One of them, Dhū al-Fiqār, in fact declared himself independent of the Ṣafavids. The young Shah Ṭahmāsp I, the son of Ismāʿīl, retook Baghdad in 1529 and gave it to Muḥammad Sultan Khan Takkalū.

In 1533 Selim's son, the Ottoman sultan Süleyman I (the Magnificent), set out on his campaign against "the Two Iraqs." In November 1534 he took Baghdad from the Ṣafavid governor Muḥammad Sultan Khan. The city was then integrated into the Ottoman Empire, except for a brief Ṣafavid reoccupation from 1623 to 1638. Lower Iraq too was incorporated into the empire by the middle of the 16th century. As a result of the Ottoman conquest, Iraq underwent complete geopolitical reorientation westward.

OTTOMAN IRAQ (1534–1918)

Ottoman Iraq was roughly approximate to the Arabian Iraq of the preceding era, though still without clearly defined borders. The Zagros Mountains, which separated Arabian Iraq from Persian Iraq, now lay on the Ottoman-Iranian frontier, but that frontier shifted with the fortunes of war. On the west and south, Iraq faded out somewhere in the sands of the Syrian and Arabian deserts. The incorporation of Arabian Iraq into the Ottoman Empire not only separated it from Persian Iraq but also reoriented it toward the Ottoman lands in Syria and Anatolia, with especially close ties binding the province (*eyālet*) of Diyār Bakr to the Iraqi provinces.

For administrative purposes Ottoman Iraq was divided into the three central *eyālets* of Mosul, Baghdad, and Al-Baṣrah, with the northern *eyālet* of Shahrizūr, east of the Tigris, and the southern *eyālet* of Al-Hasa, on the western coast of the Persian Gulf. These provinces only roughly reflected the geographic, linguistic, and religious divisions of Ottoman Iraq. Most of the inhabitants of Mosul and Shahrizūr in the north and northeast were Kurds and other non-Arabs. The people of the plains, marshes, and deserts were overwhelmingly Arabic-speaking. Few Turkish speakers were to be found outside Baghdad, Karkūk, and some other towns. Centuries of political upheavals, invasions, wars, and general insecurity had taken their toll on Iraq's population, especially in the urban centres. Destruction and neglect of the irrigation system had restricted settled agriculture to a few areas, the most extensive of which were between the rivers north of Baghdad and around Al-Baṣrah in the south. As much as half of the Arab and Kurdish population in the countryside was nomadic or seminomadic. Outside the towns, social organization and personal allegiances were primarily tribal, with many of the settled cultivators having retained their tribal ties. Baghdad, situated near the geographic centre, reflected within itself the division between the predominantly Shīʿite south and the largely Sunni north. Unlike the case in Anatolia and Syria, Iraq's non-Muslim communities were modest in size, but there was an active Jewish commercial and financial element in Baghdad, and Assyrian Christians were prominent in Mosul.

The 16th-Century Conquest of Iraq and the Regime Imposed by Süleyman I

The 16th-century conquest of Iraq, Syria, Egypt, and the Hejaz brought the holiest cities of Islam, the most important of the pilgrimage routes, and all the former seats of the caliphate under Ottoman rule and thereby reinforced the dynasty's claim to supreme leadership within the Sunni Muslim world. In Iraq, Ottoman rule represented the victory of Sunnism. Although the Shīʿite notables of southern Iraq continued to enjoy considerable local influence and prestige, they were inclined to identify with Shīʿite Iran and to resent the Sunni-dominated Ottoman administration. Control of the trade routes passing through the Red Sea and up the Tigris and Euphrates rivers and from Iran to Anatolia, Syria, and the Mediterranean was an important element in the sultan's efforts to ensure that east-west trade would continue to flow through his territories in spite of the newly opened sea routes around Africa. But, perhaps most important, Iraq served as a buffer zone, a shield protecting Ottoman Anatolia and Syria against encroachments from Iran or by the intractable Arab and Kurdish tribes.

Süleyman's imposition of direct rule over Iraq involved such traditional Ottoman administrative devices as the appointment of governors and judges, the stationing of

Janissaries, members of an elite military corps meant to reinforce the power of Ottoman sultans, became a significant political force and often challenged power through coups. The Bridgeman Art Library/Getty Images

Janissaries (elite soldiers) in the provincial capitals, and the ordering of cadastral surveys. *Timars* (military fiefs), however, were few except in some areas in the north. Although the pasha of Baghdad was accorded a certain preeminence as governor of the most important city in Ottoman Iraq (as was the governor of Damascus in Syria), this in no way implied the unity of the five *eyālets*.

The Local Despotisms in the 17th Century

In the 17th century the weakening of the central authority of the Ottoman government gave rise to local despotisms in the Iraqi provinces, as it did elsewhere in the empire. A tribal dynasty, the Banū Khālid, ruled Al-Hasa as governors from the late 16th century to 1663. In 1612 Afrāsiyāb, a military man of uncertain origin, purchased the governorship of Al-Baṣrah, which remained in his family until 1668. With the permission and even the encouragement of these autonomous governors, British, Dutch, and Portuguese merchants who were already actively involved in Red Sea trade gained a strong foothold in Al-Baṣrah.

An officer and faction leader of the Janissary garrison in Baghdad, Bakr Ṣū Bāshī, revolted in the early 17th century and negotiated with the Ṣafavid Shah ʿAbbās I to strengthen his position. In the ensuing struggle, the Ottomans managed to retain control over Mosul and Shahrizūr, but central Iraq, including Baghdad, was under Ṣafavid rule from 1623 until the Ottoman sultan Murad IV drove the Iranians out again in 1638. Whereas the Ṣafavid occupation of Baghdad had been accompanied by the destruction of some Sunni mosques and other buildings and had resulted in death or slavery for several thousand people, mostly Sunnis, many of the city's

Shīʿite inhabitants lost their lives when the Ottomans returned to Baghdad.

The Treaty of Qaṣr-e Shīrīn (also called the Treaty of Zuhāb) of 1639 brought an end to 150 years of intermittent warfare between the Ottomans and Ṣafavids and established a boundary between the two empires that remained virtually unchanged into modern times. Ottoman sovereignty had been restored in Baghdad, but the stability of central Iraq continued to be disturbed by turbulent garrison troops and by Arab and Kurdish tribal unrest. In the south too, even though the autonomous rule of the Afrāsiyāb dynasty was ended in 1668, Ottoman authority was soon challenged by the Muntafiq and Ḥawīza tribes of desert and marsh Arabs. Iranians took advantage of this disturbed state of affairs to infiltrate southern Iraq. Only after the Ottomans suffered defeat in a European war and negotiated the Treaty of Carlowitz in 1699 was the sultan able to dispatch troops to Iraq and recover Al-Baṣrah.

Developments in Iraq in the mid- and late 17th century reflected the disordered state of affairs in Istanbul. The energetic and effective reign of Murad IV was followed by that of the incompetent İbrahim I (1640–48), known as "Deli (the Mad) Ibrahim," who was eventually deposed and strangled and was succeeded by his six-year-old son, Mehmed IV (ruled 1648–87). The protracted crisis in the capital had an unsettling effect everywhere in the empire, undoing the reforms of Murad IV and bringing political and economic chaos.

The 18th-Century Mamlūk Regime

The early 18th century was a time of important changes both in Istanbul and in Baghdad. The reign of Sultan Ahmed III (1703–30) was marked by relative political stability in the capital and by extensive reforms—some influenced by European models—implemented during the "Tulip Period" (Lâle Devri, 1718–30) by Grand Vizier İbrahim Paşa.

In Baghdad, Hasan Paşa (1704–24), the Ottoman governor of Georgian origin sent from Istanbul, and his son Ahmed Paşa (1724–47) established a Georgian mamlūk (slave) household, through which they exercised authority and administered the province. The mamlūks (Turkish: *kölemen*) were mostly Christian slaves from the Caucasus who converted to Islam, were trained in a special school, and were then assigned to military and administrative duties. Hasan Paşa made himself indispensable to the Ottoman government by curbing the unruly tribes and regularly remitting tribute to the treasury in Istanbul, and Ahmed Paşa played a crucial role in defending Iraq against yet another Iranian military threat. These pashas extended their authority beyond the *eyālet* of Baghdad to include Mārdīn, 'Urfa, and much of Kurdish Shahrizūr and thus dominated the northern trade routes and secured additional sources of revenue. They also held sway over Al-Baṣrah and the trade lanes leading to the Persian Gulf, Arabia, and India. Mosul retained its separate provincial status and from 1726 to 1834 was governed by members of the powerful Jalīlī family. But, whereas the Jalīlīs, whose relationship to the sultan had some characteristics of vassalage, regularly made military contributions to Ottoman campaigns beyond their provincial frontiers, the pashas of Baghdad did not. The military forces at their disposal remained in Iraq, guarding against tribal unrest and threats from Iran.

After the collapse of Ṣafavid power in 1722, first the Afghans and later Nādir Shah (ruled 1736–47) seized power in Iran, which led to a resumption of hostilities in Ottoman Iraq. In 1733, before assuming the title of shah, Nādir unsuccessfully besieged Baghdad. He also failed to capture Mosul in 1742, and a settlement was reached in 1746 that confirmed the terms of the Treaty of Qaṣr-e Shīrīn. The assistance provided by the pashas of Baghdad and Mosul in countering the Iranian threat further enhanced their value in the eyes of the sultan's government and improved their position in their respective provinces.

When Ahmed Paşa died in 1747, shortly after the death of Nādir Shah, his mamlūks constituted a powerful, self-perpetuating elite corps of some 2,000 men. After attempts to prevent these mamlūks from assuming power failed, the Ottomans were obliged to accept their rule. By 1750 Süleyman Abū Layla, son-in-law of Ahmed Paşa and already governor of Al-Baṣrah, had reentered Baghdad and been recognized as the first Mamlūk pasha of Iraq.

In the second half of the 18th century, Iraqi political history is largely the story of the autonomous Georgian Mamlūk regime. This regime succeeded in suppressing revolts, curbed the power of the Janissaries, and restored order and some degree of prosperity to the region. In addition, it countered the Muntafiq threats in the south and made Al-Baṣrah a virtual dependency of Baghdad. Following the example set by the Afrāsiyābs in the preceding century, the Mamlūks encouraged European trade by permitting the British East India Company to establish an agency in Al-Baṣrah in 1763. Their failure to develop a regular system of succession and the gradual formation of several competing Mamlūk households, however, resulted in factionalism and instability, which proved advantageous to a new ruler of Iran.

Karīm Khan Zand ended the anarchy after Nādir Shāh's assassination and from 1765 ruled over most of Iran from Shīrāz. Like the Mamlūk rulers of Iraq, he was interested in the economic returns derived from fostering European trade in the Persian Gulf. His brother, Ṣādiq Khan, took Al-Baṣrah in 1776 after a protracted and stubborn resistance directed by its Mamlūk governor, Süleyman Ağa, and held it until Karīm Khan's death in 1779. Süleyman then returned from Shīrāz, where he had been held captive, and in 1780 was given the governorship of Baghdad, Al-Baṣrah, and Shahrizūr by Sultan Abdülhamid I (ruled 1774–89). He was known as Büyük (the Great) Süleyman Paşa, and his rule (1780–1802) is generally acknowledged to represent the apogee of Mamlūk power in Iraq. He imported large numbers of mamlūks to strengthen his own household, curbed the factionalism among rival households, eliminated the Janissaries as an independent local force, and fostered trade and agriculture. His attempts to control the Arab Bedouin were less successful, and Wahhābī incursions from Arabia into Al-Hasa and along the fringes of the desert, climaxing in the sack of the Shīʿite shrine at Karbalā' in 1801, added to his difficulties.

British East India Company

The British East India Company—also called English East India Company, known formally as Governor and Company of Merchants of London Trading into the East Indies (1600–1708) or United Company of Merchants of England Trading to the East Indies (1708–1873)—was an English company formed for the exploitation of trade with East and Southeast Asia and India, incorporated by royal charter on Dec. 31, 1600. Starting as a monopolistic trading body, the company became involved in politics and acted as an agent of British imperialism in India from the early 18th century to the mid-19th century. In addition, the activities of the company in China in the 19th century served as a catalyst for the expansion of British influence there.

The company was formed to share in the East Indian spice trade. This trade had been a monopoly of Spain and Portugal until the defeat of the Spanish Armada (1588) by England gave the English the chance to break the monopoly. Until 1612 the company conducted separate voyages, separately subscribed. There were temporary joint stocks until 1657, when a permanent joint stock was raised.

The company met with opposition from the Dutch in the Dutch East Indies (now Indonesia) and the Portuguese. The Dutch virtually excluded company members from the East Indies after the Amboina Massacre in 1623 (an incident in which English, Japanese, and Portuguese traders were executed by Dutch authorities), but the company's defeat of the Portuguese in India (1612) won them trading concessions from the Mughal Empire. The company settled down to a trade in cotton and silk piece goods, indigo, and saltpetre, with spices from South India. It extended its activities to the Persian Gulf, Southeast Asia, and East Asia.

After the mid-18th century the cotton goods trade declined, while tea became an important import from China. Beginning in the early 19th century, the company financed the tea trade with illegal opium exports to China. Chinese opposition to this trade precipitated the first Opium War (1839–42), which resulted in a Chinese defeat and the expansion of British trading privileges. A second conflict, often called the "Arrow" War (1856–60), brought increased trading rights for Europeans.

The original company faced opposition to its monopoly, which led to the establishment of a rival company and the fusion (1708) of the two as the United Company of Merchants of England trading to the East Indies. The United Company was organized into a court of 24 directors who worked through committees. They were elected annually by the Court of Proprietors, or shareholders. When the company acquired control of Bengal in 1757, Indian policy was until 1773 influenced by shareholders' meetings, where votes could be bought by the purchase of shares. This led to government intervention. The Regulating Act (1773) and Pitt's India Act (1784) established government control of political policy through a regulatory board responsible to Parliament. Thereafter, the company gradually lost both commercial and political control. Its commercial monopoly was broken in 1813, and from 1834 it was merely a managing agency for the British government of India. It was deprived of this after the Indian Mutiny (1857), and it ceased to exist as a legal entity in 1873.

The Fall of the Mamlūks and the Consolidation of British Interests

Britain's influence in Iraq had received a major boost in 1798 when Süleyman Paşa gave permission for a permanent British agent to be appointed in Baghdad. This increasing European penetration and the restoration of direct Ottoman rule, accompanied by military, administrative, and other reforms, are the dominant features of 19th-century Iraqi history. The last Mamlūk governor of Iraq, Dā'ūd Paşa (1816–31), turned increasingly to Europe for weapons and advisers to equip and train his military force and endeavoured to improve communications and promote trade. In this respect he resembled his contemporary in Egypt, Muḥammad 'Alī Paşa. But, whereas Muḥammad 'Alī's Egypt drew closer to France, it was Great Britain that continued to strengthen its position in the Persian Gulf and Iraq.

The fall of Dā'ūd can be attributed in part to the determination of Sultan Mahmud II (ruled 1808–39) to curtail provincial autonomy and restore the central authority of his government throughout the realm. Dā'ūd's removal, however, was facilitated by opposition within Iraq to the Mamlūk regime and, more immediately, by the floods that devastated Baghdad in 1831 and the plague that decimated its population in the same year. The Mamlūks had always been obliged to share power, to one extent or another, with groups of local notables—tribal sheikhs in the countryside and urban-based groups associated with the garrison troops, the bureaucracy, the merchants, or the religious elite. The last of these included not only high-ranking legal officials and scholars but also the heads of Sufi orders, the prominent noble (*ashrāf*) families, and the custodians of the great religious shrines—both Sunni and Shī'ite. Nor were the Mamlūk pashas of Baghdad ever so independent of the sultan's government as it has sometimes been made to appear. Dā'ūd was not the first to be deposed by force. They usually paid tribute and, through their representatives in the capital, frequently distributed "gifts" to high officials in the palace and at the Sublime Porte who might assist in securing their reappointment.

The arrival of a new Ottoman governor in Baghdad in 1831 signaled the end of the Mamlūk period and the beginning of a new era in Iraq. Direct rule was gradually imposed over the region. The Jalīlīs of Mosul submitted in 1834; the Bābān family of Al-Sulaymāniyyah followed suit in 1850 when Ottoman forces subjugated the Kurdish area; and by the 1850s the independent power of the Shīʿite religious elites of Karbalā' and Al-Najaf had been curtailed. To exercise some control in the tribal areas, the Ottomans continued to rely on the traditional methods of intervening in the competition for tribal leadership, making alliances, pitting one tribal group against another, and occasionally using military force. While the Arab and Kurdish tribes remained a problem, the reforms set in motion by the Ottomans did affect the tribal structure of Iraq and alleviate the problem to some extent.

Mid-19th-Century Ottoman Reforms

The military reforms undertaken by Mahmud II after the Janissary corps was destroyed in 1826 were gradually extended to Iraq. The Iraqi Janissary regiments were reorganized and, together with new troops sent from the capital and soldiers recruited locally as military conscription was applied in various parts of Iraq, formed what later became the Ottoman 6th Army. So many Iraqis opted for a military career that, by the end of the 19th century, they formed the most numerous group of Arab officers in the Ottoman army. Most

When the Iraqi Janissary regiments were combined with new and recruited troops and soldiers, they formed what would become the Ottoman 6th Army. Buyenlarge/Archive Photos/Getty Images

were Sunnis from modest families, educated in military schools set up in Baghdad and other provincial cities by the Ottoman government. Some were then admitted to the military academy in Istanbul, such as Nūrī al-Sa'īd and Yāsīn al-Hāshimī, who became leading figures in the post-World War I state of Iraq.

Apart from the military schools and the traditional religious schools, a number of primary and secondary schools were opened by the government and by foreign Roman Catholic, Protestant, and Jewish missionary organizations. In 1865 the Alliance Israélite Universelle founded what is reputed to have been the best school in Baghdad, and its graduates contributed to the great advances made by the Iraqi Jewish community during the next half century. Graduates of the government schools were expected to enter the provincial bureaucracy, and most did so. Some members of local notable families, among them the Jalīlīs of Mosul and the Bābāns of Al-Sulaymāniyyah, chose careers in administration, but it was Turkish speakers from Karkūk and descendants of the Caucasian Mamlūks who were especially well represented in the bureaucratic ranks. The highest administrative posts, however, were filled by appointees from Istanbul.

As secular reforms were implemented and the role of the state expanded in the 19th century, Iraqi religious notables and officeholders—both Shīʿite and Sunni—suffered a relative loss of status, influence, and wealth. Meanwhile, Ottoman civil administrators and army officers, virtually all of whom were Sunnis, came to constitute a political elite that carried over into post-1918 Iraq.

Along with new military, administrative, and educational institutions, the communications network was expanded and modernized. Steamships first appeared on the Tigris and Euphrates in 1835, and a company was later formed to provide regular service between Al-Baṣrah and Baghdad. To handle the increasing volume of trade, the port facilities of Al-Baṣrah were developed. In the 1860s telegraph lines linked Baghdad with Istanbul, and in the 1880s the postal system was extended to Iraq. Roads were improved and new ones were built. Railroad construction, however, did not begin until the Germans built the Baghdad-to-Sāmarrāʾ line just before World War I.

The Governorship of Midhat Paşa

The most dramatic and far-reaching changes in Iraq are associated with the introduction of the new Ottoman provincial system and the governorship of Midhat Paşa (1869–72). Midhat was one of the chief architects of the

Ottoman Vilayet Law of 1864, and he had applied it with great success to a *vilayet* elsewhere in the empire before arriving in Baghdad in 1869 with a handpicked corps of advisers and assistants.

Midhat transformed the face of Baghdad by ordering the demolition of a section of the old city wall to allow room for rational urban expansion. He established a tramway to suburban Kāẓimayn, a public park, a water-supply system, a hospital, textile mills, a savings bank, paved and lighted streets, and the only bridge across the Tigris built in the city until the 20th century. Several new schools were opened; modern textbooks were printed on the press that Midhat founded; and Iraq's first newspaper, *Al-Zawrāʾ*, began publication. To develop the economy he promoted regular steamer service on the Tigris and Euphrates and shipping in the Persian Gulf, set up ship-repair yards at Al-Baṣrah, began dredging operations on the Shatt al-Arab, made some minor improvements in the irrigation system, and expanded date production in the south. Municipalities and administrative councils were established in accordance with the new *vilayet* regulations, and military conscription was enforced.

But perhaps the most fundamental changes resulted from Midhat's attempt to apply the Ottoman Land Law of 1858, which aimed at classifying and regularizing land tenure and registering land titles to individuals who would be responsible for paying the applicable taxes. His objectives were to pacify and settle the tribes, encourage cultivation, and improve tax collection. However, the traditional system of tribal and communal landholding and the fear that land registration would lead to greater government control, heavier tax burdens, and extension of military conscription to the tribal areas—combined with inefficient and inequitable administration—limited the effectiveness of the reform and produced unintended results. Most land was registered not in the names of individual peasants and tribesmen but rather in the names of tribal sheikhs, urban-based merchants, and former tax farmers. Some tribal leaders became landlords, which tied them more closely to the Ottoman administration and widened the gap between them and their tribesmen. Other sheikhs refused to cooperate. A combination of developments stemming from the reforms begun by Midhat Paşa resulted in a decline of nomadism in Iraq. The proportion of nomads fell from about one-third of the population in 1867 to approximately half that figure by the end of the Ottoman period.

Midhat's authority as *vali* (governor) of Baghdad and commander of the Ottoman 6th Army extended north to include Mosul, Karkūk, and Al-Sulaymāniyyah. In 1871 Midhat, in cooperation with Sheikh ʿAbd Allāh al-Sabāḥ, ruler of Kuwait, sent an expeditionary force to occupy Al-Hasa (which was situated along the coast south of Kuwait), which thereby gave Midhat effective control of Al-Hasa and Al-Baṣrah in the south. In recognition of his cooperation, ʿAbd Allāh was appointed an Ottoman *qāʾim-maqām* (subgovernor), although Kuwait remained independent throughout the entire Ottoman period and acknowledged Ottoman suzerainty only as a formality. Taking advantage of divisions within the Saʿūd family, Midhat also sought to reassert Ottoman sovereignty over the Wahhābī dominions in the Najd region of central Arabia. His success in the latter effort was ephemeral, as were many of the projects begun by Midhat. Nevertheless, his brief rule set in motion developments that profoundly changed virtually every aspect of life in Iraq and tied it more closely to Istanbul than ever before.

The End of Ottoman Rule

In the last decades of Ottoman rule, changes in administrative boundaries once more split Ottoman Iraq into three parts. For most of this period, both Al-Baṣrah (together with the subprovince [*sanjak*] of Al-Hasa) and Mosul (and its dependent *sanjaks* of Karkūk and Al-Sulaymāniyyah) were *vilayets* independent of the central province of Baghdad.

In spite of the European commercial and consular presence in Iraq, it remained more isolated from European influences than the Arab lands adjacent to the Mediterranean. Iraq had relatively few Christians, and those few had had little exposure to foreign ideas. The prosperous Jewish community usually avoided politics but tended to be favourably disposed toward the Ottoman government. The tribal sheikhs and Shīʿite notables still couched their opposition in traditional terms, and many Turkish and Caucasian families enjoyed official status and other rewards as provincial administrators. Finally, a great majority of the population was illiterate. Thus, it is hardly surprising that Arab nationalism had made little impact on Iraq before World War I. In Syria, Arab nationalist and separatist organizations appeared after the Young Turk Revolution of 1908. In Iraq, however, there was scant nationalist opposition to Ottoman rule, although some Iraqi Arab officers in the Ottoman army joined the secret al-ʿAhd ("Covenant") society, which is reported to have advocated independence for the sultan's Arab provinces.

It was the British, whose interests in the Persian Gulf and the Tigris-Euphrates region had grown steadily since the late 18th century, who ultimately brought an end to the Ottoman presence in Iraq. In the years just before World War I, the close ties between the governments of the kaiser in Berlin and the Young Turks in Istanbul were particularly troublesome to Great Britain. When Germany was awarded a concession to extend its railway line through Anatolia to Baghdad and acquired mineral rights to the land on both sides of the proposed route, heightened fear of German competition in Iraq and the Persian Gulf evoked strong protests from London. Soon afterward, the Anglo-Persian Oil Company (later the British Petroleum Company PLC) began production on the Iranian side of the gulf, and there were indications that oil might be found elsewhere in the area. In 1912 a group representing British, German, and Dutch interests formed the Turkish Petroleum Company, which, on the eve of the war, was given a concession to explore for oil in the *vilayets* of Mosul and Baghdad. A convention between Britain and the Ottoman Empire acknowledging British protection of Kuwait was concluded in 1913 but was never ratified. In view of these developments and because they feared that the Germans might persuade the Ottomans to undertake military action against them, the British had already made plans to send an expedition from India to protect their interests in the Persian Gulf before the Ottoman Empire entered the war in early November 1914. After war was declared, a British expeditionary force soon landed at the head of the gulf and on Nov. 22, 1914, entered Al-Baṣrah. In a campaign aimed at taking Baghdad, the British suffered a defeat at Al-Kūt (Kūt al-ʿAmārah) in April 1916, but a reinforced British army marched into Baghdad on March 11, 1917. An administration staffed largely by British and Indian officials replaced the Ottoman provincial government in occupied Iraq, but Mosul remained in Ottoman hands until after the Armistice of Mudros (Oct. 30, 1918), which brought an end to the war in the Middle East. Under the Treaty of Lausanne (1923), Turkey (the successor to the Ottoman Empire) gave up all claims to its former Arab provinces, including Iraq.

Armistice of Mudros

The Armistice of Mudros (Oct. 30, 1918), a pact signed at the port of Mudros, on the Aegean island of Lemnos, between the Ottoman Empire and Great Britain (representing the Allied powers), marked the defeat of the Ottoman Empire in World War I (1914–18). Under the terms of the armistice, the Ottomans surrendered their remaining garrisons in Hejaz, Yemen, Syria, Mesopotamia, Tripolitania, and Cyrenaica; the Allies were to occupy the Straits of the Dardanelles and the Bosporus, Batum (now in southwest Georgia), and the Taurus tunnel system; and the Allies won the right to occupy "in case of disorder" the six Armenian provinces in Anatolia and to seize "any strategic points" in case of a threat to Allied security. The Ottoman army was demobilized, and Turkish ports, railways, and other strategic points were made available for use by the Allies.

IRAQ UNTIL THE 1958 REVOLUTION

Merging the three provinces of Mosul, Baghdad, and Al-Baṣrah into one political entity and creating a nation out of the diverse religious and ethnic elements inhabiting these lands were accomplished after World War I. Action undertaken by the British military authorities during the war and the upsurge of nationalism afterward helped determine the shape of the new Iraqi state and the course of events during the postwar years until Iraq finally emerged as an independent political entity in 1932.

British Occupation and the Mandatory Regime

British control of Iraq was short-lived. After the war Britain debated both its general policy in Iraq and the specific type of administration to establish. Two schools of thought influenced policy makers in London. The first, advocated by the Colonial Office, stressed a policy of direct control to protect British interests in the Persian Gulf and India. Assessing British policy from India, this school may be called the Indian school of thought. The other school, hoping to conciliate Arab nationalists, advised indirect control. In Iraq itself British authorities were divided on the issue. Some, under the influence of Sir Arnold Wilson, the acting civil commissioner, advocated direct control. Others, alarmed by growing dissatisfaction with the British administration, advised indirect control and suggested the establishment of an indigenous regime under British supervision. Britain was still undecided on which policy it should follow in 1920 when events in other Arab countries radically changed conditions in Iraq.

Early in 1920 the emir Fayṣal I, son of the sharif Ḥusayn ibn ʿAlī (then king of the Hejaz), who had led the Arab Revolt of 1916 against the Ottomans, established an Arab government in Damascus and was proclaimed king of Syria. Meanwhile, a group of Iraqi nationalists met in Damascus to proclaim the emir ʿAbd Allāh, older brother of Fayṣal, king of Iraq. Under the influence of nationalist activities in Syria, nationalist agitation followed first in northern Iraq and then in the tribal areas of the middle Euphrates. By the summer of 1920, the revolt had spread to all parts of the country except the big cities of Mosul, Baghdad, and Al-Baṣrah, where British forces were stationed.

In July 1920 Fayṣal came into conflict with the French authorities over control of Syria. France had been given the mandate over Syria and Lebanon in April and was determined to obtain Fayṣal's acceptance of the mandate. Nationalists urged Fayṣal to reject the French demands, and the conflict that ensued between him and the French resulted in his expulsion from Syria. Fayṣal went to London

Emir Fayṣal I was a statesman and king of Iraq. He helped advance Arab nationalism throughout and following World War I. Evening Standard/ Hulton Archive/Getty Images

to complain about the French action.

Although the revolt in Iraq was suppressed by force, it prompted Iraq and Great Britain to reconcile their differences. In Britain a segment of public opinion wanted to "get out of Mesopotamia" and urged relief from further commitments. In Iraq the nationalists were demanding independence. In 1921 Britain offered the Iraqi throne to Fayṣal along with the establishment of an Arab government under British mandate. Fayṣal wanted the throne if it was offered to him by the Iraqi people. He also suggested the replacement of the mandate by a treaty of alliance. These proposals were accepted by the British government, and Colonial Secretary Winston Churchill promised to carry them out. He was advised by T.E. Lawrence, known for his sympathy for the Arabs.

In March 1921 a conference presided over by Churchill was held in Cairo to settle Middle Eastern affairs. Fayṣal was nominated to the Iraqi throne with the provision that a plebiscite be held to confirm the nomination. Sir Percy Cox, recently appointed a high commissioner for Iraq, was responsible for carrying out the plebiscite. A provisional government set up by Cox shortly before the Cairo

Conference passed a resolution in July 1921 declaring Fayṣal king of Iraq, provided that his "Government shall be constitutional, representative and democratic." The plebiscite confirmed this proclamation, and Fayṣal was formally crowned king on August 23.

The establishment of the monarchy was the first step in setting up a national regime. Two other steps followed immediately: the signing of a treaty of alliance with Great Britain and the drafting of a constitution. It was deemed necessary that a treaty precede the constitution and define relations between Iraq and Britain. The treaty was signed on Oct. 10, 1922. Without direct reference it reproduced most of the provisions of the mandate. Iraq undertook to respect religious freedom and missionary enterprises and the rights of foreigners, to treat all states equally, and to cooperate with the League of Nations. Britain was obligated to offer advice on foreign and domestic affairs, such as military, judicial, and financial matters (defined in separate and subsidiary agreements). Although the terms of the treaty were open to periodic revision, they were to last 20 years. In the meantime, Britain agreed to prepare Iraq for membership in the League of Nations "as soon as possible."

It soon became apparent that the substance, though not the form, of the mandate was still in existence and that complete independence had not been achieved. Strong opposition to the treaty in the press made it almost certain that it would not be ratified by Iraq's Constituent Assembly. Nor was British public opinion satisfied with the commitments to Iraq. During the general elections of 1922, there was a newspaper campaign against British expenditures in Iraq. In deference to public opinion in both Britain and Iraq, a protocol to the treaty was signed in April 1923, reducing the period of the treaty from 20 to 4 years. In spite of the shortening of British tutelage, the

Constituent Assembly demanded complete independence when the treaty was put before it for approval. Ratification of the treaty was accomplished in June 1924, after Britain's warning that if it was not approved, the matter would be referred to the League of Nations.

The Constituent Assembly then considered a draft constitution drawn up by a constitutional committee. The committee tried to give extensive powers to the king. Discussion on the draft constitution by the Constituent Assembly lasted a month, and after minor modifications it was adopted in July 1924. The Organic Law, as the constitution was called, went into effect right after it was signed by the king in March 1925. It provided for a constitutional monarchy, a parliamentary government, and a bicameral legislature. The latter was composed of an elected House of Representatives and an appointed Senate. The lower house was to be elected every four years in a free manhood suffrage. The first Parliament met in 1925. Ten general elections were held before the downfall of the monarchy in 1958. The more than 50 cabinets formed during the same period reflected the instability of the system.

From the establishment of a national government, there was keen interest in organizing political parties. Three parties formed in 1921, one by the group in power and two by opposition parties, had similar social and economic views and essentially the same political objective: terminating the mandate and winning independence. They differed, however, on the means of realizing the objective. After the achievement of independence in 1932, these parties dissolved, because their raison d'être had disappeared. It was only when social issues were discussed that new political groupings, even if not formally organized as political parties, began to emerge. The power struggle between these groups became exceedingly intense after World War II (1939–45).

The Iraqi nationalists, though appreciating the free expression of opinion permitted under a parliamentary system, were far from satisfied with the mandate. They demanded independence as a matter of right, as promised in war declarations and treaties, rather than as a matter of capacity for self-government as laid down in the mandate. Various attempts were made to redefine Anglo-Iraqi relations, as embodied in the 1926 and 1927 treaties, without fundamentally altering Britain's responsibility. The British treaties were viewed by the nationalists not only as an impediment to the realization of Iraq's nationalist aspirations but also as inimical to the economic development of the country. The nationalists viewed the situation as a "perplexing predicament" (*al-waḍʿ al-shādh*)—a term that became popular in Parliament and in the press. It referred to the impossibility of government by the dual authority of the mandate. The nationalists argued that there were two governments in Iraq, one foreign and the other national, and that such a regime was an abnormality that, though feasible in theory, was unworkable in practice.

In 1929 Britain decided to end this stalemate and reconcile its interests with Iraq's national aspirations. It notified Iraq that the mandate would be terminated in 1932, and a new treaty of independence was negotiated. A new government was formed, headed by Gen. Nūrī al-Saʿīd, who helped in achieving Iraq's independence.

The new treaty was signed in June 1930. It provided for the establishment of a "close alliance" between Britain and Iraq with "full and frank consultation between them in all matters of foreign policy which may affect their common interests." Iraq would maintain internal order and defend itself against foreign aggression, supported by Britain. Any dispute between Iraq and a third state involving the risk of war was to be discussed with Britain in the hope of a settlement in accordance with the Covenant of the League of Nations. In the event of an imminent threat of war, the two parties would take a common defense position. Iraq recognized that the maintenance and protection of essential British communications was in the interest of both parties. Air-base sites for British troops were therefore granted near Al-Baṣrah and west of the Euphrates, but these forces "shall not constitute in any manner an occupation, and will in no way prejudice the sovereign rights of Iraq." This treaty, valid for 25 years, was to go into effect after Iraq joined the League of Nations.

In 1932, when Iraq was still under British control, the boundaries between Iraq and Kuwait were clearly defined in an exchange of letters between the two governments, but they were never ratified by Iraq in accordance with the Iraqi constitution. This set the stage for future Iraqi claims on Kuwaiti territory, particularly on the islands of Būbiyān and Warbah, which had originally been part of the Ottoman province of Al-Baṣrah but had been ceded to Kuwait in the unratified convention of 1913.

Independence, 1932–39

On Oct. 3, 1932, Iraq was admitted to the League of Nations as an independent state. Because conflict between Iraq's political leaders centred essentially on how to end the mandate rather than on the right of independence, King Fayṣal sought the cooperation of opposition leaders after independence. Shortly after Iraq's admission to the League, Nūrī al-Saʿīd, who had been prime minister since 1930, resigned. After an interim administration, King Fayṣal invited Rashīd ʿAlī al-Gaylānī, one of the opposition leaders, to form a new government. For a short while it seemed that all the country's leaders would close ranks and devote all their efforts to internal reforms.

But internal dissension soon developed. The first incident was the Assyrian uprising of 1933. The Assyrians, a small Christian community living in Mosul province, were given assurances of security by both Britain and Iraq. When the mandate was ended, the Assyrians began to feel insecure and demanded new assurances. Matters came to a head in the summer of 1933 when King Fayṣal was in Europe. The opposition, now in power, wanted to impress the public through a high-handed policy toward a minority group. In clashes with the Iraqi troops, several hundred Assyrians were brutally killed. The incident was brought to the attention of the League of Nations less than a year after Iraq had given assurances that it would protect minority rights. Had King Fayṣal been in the country, he likely would have counseled moderation. Upon his hasty return to Baghdad, he found deep-seated divisions and a situation beyond his control. Suffering from heart trouble, he returned to Switzerland, where he died in September 1933. The Assyrian incident brought about the fall of Rashīd ʿAlī and his replacement by a moderate government.

Fayṣal was succeeded by his son, King Ghāzī (ruled 1933–39), who was young and inexperienced—a situation that gave political leaders an opportunity to compete for power. Without political parties to channel their activities through constitutional processes, politicians resorted to extraconstitutional, or violent, methods. One method was to embarrass those in power by press attacks, palace intrigues, or incidents that would cause cabinet dissension and force the prime minister to resign. The first five governmental changes after independence, from 1932 to 1934, were produced by these methods.

Another tactic was to incite tribal uprisings in areas where there were tribal chiefs unfriendly to the group in power. Tribes, though habitually opposed to authority, had been brought under control and remained relatively quiet after 1932. When opposition leaders began to incite them against the government in 1934, however, they rebelled and caused the fall of three governments from 1934 to 1935.

A third method was military intervention. The opposition would try to obtain the loyalty of army officers, plan a coup d'état, and force those in power to resign. This method, often resorted to by the opposition, proved to be the most dangerous because, once the army intervened in politics, it became increasingly difficult to reestablish civilian rule. From 1936 until 1941, when it was defeated in a war with Britain, the army dominated domestic politics. (The army again intervened in 1958 and remained the dominant force in politics until the rise of the Baʿth Party 10 years later.)

Two different sets of opposition leaders produced the first military coup, in 1936. The first group, led by Ḥikmat Sulaymān, was a faction of old politicians who sought power by violent methods. The other was the Ahālī group, composed mainly of young men who advocated socialism and democracy and sought to carry out reform programs. It was Ḥikmat Sulaymān, however, who urged Gen. Bakr Ṣidqī, commander of an army division, to stage a surprise attack on Baghdad in cooperation with another military commander and forced the cabinet to resign. Apparently, King Ghāzī was also disenchanted with the group in power and so allowed the government to resign. Ḥikmat Sulaymān became prime minister in October 1936, and Bakr Ṣidqī was appointed chief of general staff. Neither the Ahālī group nor Ḥikmat Sulaymān could improve social conditions, however, because the army gradually dominated the political scene. Supported by opposition leaders, a dissident military faction assassinated Bakr Ṣidqī, but civilian rule was not reestablished. This first military coup introduced a new factor in politics. Lack of leadership after the assassination of Bakr Ṣidqī left the army divided, while jealousy among leading army officers induced each faction to support a different set of civilian leaders. The army became virtually the deciding factor in cabinet changes and remained so until 1941.

In spite of political instability, material progress continued during King Ghāzī's short reign. Oil had been discovered near Karkūk in 1927, and, by the outbreak of World War II, oil revenue had begun to play an important role in domestic spending and added a new facet to Iraq's foreign relations. The Al-Kūt irrigation project, begun in 1934, was completed, and other projects, to be financed by oil royalties, were planned. The pipelines from the Karkūk oil fields to the Mediterranean were opened in 1935. The railroads, still under British control, were purchased in 1935, and the Baʿījī-Tal Küçük section, the only missing railway link between the Persian Gulf and Europe, was completed in 1938. There was also a noticeable increase in construction, foreign trade, and educational facilities. Several disputes with neighbouring countries were settled, including one over the boundary with Syria, which was concluded in Iraq's favour; Iraq thereafter possessed the Sinjār Mountains. A nonaggression pact, called the Saʿdābād Pact, between Turkey, Iran, Afghanistan, and Iraq was signed in 1937. In 1939, shortly before the outbreak of World War II, King Ghāzī was killed in a car accident, and his son Fayṣal II ascended the throne. As Fayṣal was only four years old, his uncle, Emir ʿAbd al-Ilāh, was appointed regent and served in this capacity for the next 14 years.

World War II and British Intervention, 1939–45

Nūrī al-Saʿīd, author of the 1930 treaty, was prime minister when war broke out. Believing that the Anglo-Iraqi alliance was the best guarantee for Iraqi security, he wanted to declare war on Germany, but his ministers counseled caution, as British victory was then in doubt. The premier accordingly declared Iraq nonbelligerent and severed diplomatic relations with Germany. When Italy entered the war in 1940, however, Nūrī al-Saʿīd, then minister of foreign affairs in the cabinet of newly appointed prime minister Rashīd ʿAlī al-Gaylānī, was unable to persuade the cabinet to break off diplomatic relations with Italy. Under the influence of pan-Arab leaders, public opinion in Iraq changed radically after France's fall, becoming especially hostile to Britain because other Arab countries remained under foreign control. Pan-Arabs urged Iraqi leaders to free Syria and Palestine and achieve unity among Arab countries. Extremists advocated alliance with Germany as the country that would foster independence and unity among Arabs.

Rashīd ʿAlī was at first unwilling to side with the extremists and gave lip service to the Anglo-Iraqi alliance. Dissension among the Iraqi leaders, however, forced him to side with the pan-Arabs. Leading army officers also fell under pan-Arab influences and encouraged Rashīd ʿAlī to detach Iraq from the British alliance. During 1940 and 1941, Iraqi officers were unwilling to cooperate with Britain, and the pan-Arab leaders began secret negotiations with the Axis Powers. Britain decided to send reinforcements to Iraq. Rashīd ʿAlī, while allowing a small British force to land in 1940, was forced to resign early in 1941, but he was reinstated by the army in April and refused further British requests for reinforcements.

British contingents entered Iraq from the Persian Gulf and from the Ḥabbāniyyah air base in April and May 1941; armed conflict with Iraqi forces followed. The hostilities lasted only 30 days, during which period a few Iraqi leaders, including the regent and Nūrī al-Saʿīd, fled the country. By the end of May, the Iraqi army had capitulated. Rashīd ʿAlī and his pan-Arab supporters left the country.

Nūrī al-Saʿīd

(b. 1888, Baghdad—d. July 14, 1958, Baghdad)

Nūrī al-Saʿīd was an Iraqi army officer, statesman, and political leader who maintained close ties with Great Britain and worked for Arab unity. He was commissioned in the Turkish Army in 1909, when Iraq was a province of the Ottoman Empire. During World War I (1914–18) he participated in Ottoman military operations against the British. He was soon captured by the British, however, and in 1916 he joined the Sharīfian Arab army led by Fayṣal I, which Great Britain was supporting in a revolt against Ottoman rule in the Arab provinces; Nūrī distinguished himself in battle. At the war's end Fayṣal established a short-lived Arab state, centred in Damascus, and Nūrī served actively in its administration. After the French destroyed this state in 1920, Fayṣal became the first king of Iraq (1921). Nūrī returned to occupy a number of influential positions, becoming prime minister in 1930. In this capacity Nūrī negotiated a 20-year treaty with Great Britain that, although maintaining substantial British influence, granted independence to Iraq.

Nūrī served as prime minister on 14 different occasions, remaining faithful to two dominant policies: a pro-British attitude and support of the Hāshimite dynasty, which King Fayṣal represented until his death in 1933. Neither of these beliefs was shared by the rising generation of younger army officers, and at the beginning of World War II open conflicts developed. Nūrī wished to support the British by declaring war against Germany and breaking off diplomatic relations with Italy. He was opposed by influential army officers, who in April 1941 supported a coup under the leadership of Rashīd ʿAlī al-Gaylānī. Nūrī and the king fled into exile. The British defeated the government of al-Gaylānī in open warfare, after which Nūrī returned to Iraq and served as prime minister under British sponsorship in 1941–44.

Nūrī maintained political order in Iraq while advocating a union of several Arab nations into a single state. Iraq became a charter member of the Arab League in 1945. Through tough and effective use of the police and the press, Nūrī repressed critics of the Iraqi crown and eliminated opportunities for army intervention.

Violent nationalist feeling in Iraq after World War II precluded renewal of the Anglo-Iraqi treaty, in spite of Nūrī's ardent support. In 1955 the United States sponsored the Baghdad Pact, a mutual security agreement among Middle Eastern states, and Nūrī saw Iraqi membership as a solution to the troublesome problem of the Anglo-Iraqi treaty. He hoped to induce other Arab states to join the pact and then assert leadership of the Arab unity movement and secure popular support in Iraq. Popular resentment against the West, however, had become too widespread for the Baghdad Pact to serve these ends. When Nūrī sponsored an Arab union with Jordan in February 1958 (Jordan was closely allied with the West), Iraqi army units, under the leadership of ʿAbd al-Karīm Qāsim, overthrew the monarchy. Nūrī was assassinated following the revolution of July 1958.

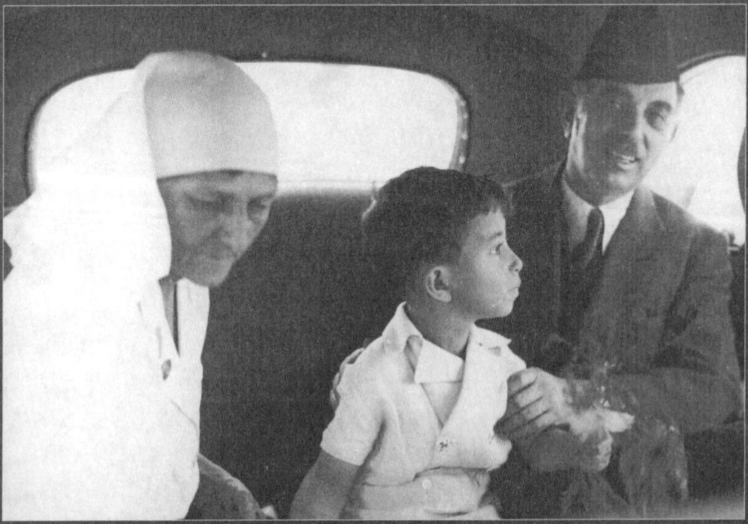

Nūrī al-Saʿīd (shown here with the young Fayṣal II) was unwavering in his determination to achieve Arab unity. Three Lions/Hulton Archive/ Getty Images

The return of the regent and moderate leaders through British intervention had far-reaching consequences. Britain was given what it demanded: the use of transportation and communication facilities and a declaration of war on the Axis Powers in January 1942. Rashīd ʿAlī's supporters were dismissed from the service, and some were interned for the duration of the war. Four officers who were responsible for the British-Iraqi conflict were hanged.

Postwar Reconstruction and Social Upheavals, 1945–58

During World War II, liberal and moderate Iraqi elements began to play an active political role. The entry of the United States and the Soviet Union into the war and their declarations in favour of democratic freedoms greatly enhanced the position of the Iraqi democratic elements. The people endured shortages and regulations restricting personal liberty and the freedom of the press, trusting that the end of the war would bring the promised better way of life. The government, however, paid no attention to the new spirit, and the wartime regulations and restrictions continued after the war. The regent, ʿAbd al-Ilāh, called a meeting of the country's leaders in 1945 and made a speech in which he attributed public disaffection to the absence of a truly parliamentary system. He called for the formation of political parties and promised full freedom for their activities and the launching of social and economic reforms.

The immediate reactions to the regent's speech were favourable, but, when political parties were formed in 1946 and certain regulations were abolished, the older politicians and vested interests resisted. The new government formed in January 1946 was overthrown within a few months of its inception. Nūrī al-Saʿīd then became prime minister and tried to enlist the cooperation of political parties, but the general elections held under his government's supervision were no different from previous controlled elections. The parties boycotted the elections. Nūrī al-Saʿīd resigned in March 1947, and Ṣāliḥ Jabr formed a new government.

Jabr, the first Shīʿite politician to become a prime minister, included in his cabinet a number of young men, but he himself was unacceptable to some liberal and nationalist elements who had been roughly handled when he was wartime minister of interior. Jabr tried to help the Arabs in Palestine in order to improve his image in nationalist circles, but he mishandled opposition leaders. Most damaging was his attempt to replace the Anglo-Iraqi treaty of 1930 without consulting with Iraqi leaders. When he was asked to consult with others, he called in only older politicians and excluded the younger leaders.

Jabr entered into negotiations with Britain with the intention of enhancing his own position. When he found that Britain wanted to retain control of its air bases in Iraq, he insisted that Britain accept the principle of Iraqi control of the bases; Iraq would allow Britain to use them in the event of war. He threatened to resign if Britain refused his proposals.

It was with this understanding that Jabr proceeded to London early in 1948 to negotiate a new treaty. He and Ernest Bevin, the British foreign secretary, quickly came to an agreement and signed a 20-year treaty at Portsmouth on Jan. 15, 1948. It provided for a new alliance between Iraq and Britain on the basis of equality and complete independence and required that "each of the high contracting parties undertake not to adopt in foreign countries an attitude which is inconsistent with the alliance or which might create difficulties for the other party." An improvement of the 1930 treaty, this document sought an alliance on the basis of mutual interests. The two air bases, which were often the subject of criticism, were returned to Iraq. British forces were to be evacuated, and Iraq would be supplied with arms and military training. The annex to the treaty stressed the importance of the air bases as "an essential element in the defense of Iraq." Britain's use of the bases in the event of war, or threat of war, would depend on Iraq's invitation. The treaty also provided for the establishment of a joint defense board for common defense and consultation. Both parties agreed to grant each other necessary facilities for defense purposes.

In spite of these advances, the treaty was repudiated immediately in a popular uprising. Street demonstrations had occurred before the treaty was signed, in defense of Arab rights in Palestine, but, when the news of the signing of the new treaty was broadcast in London, rioting and demonstrations in Baghdad followed. Within a week of the signing, the regent called a meeting at the royal household that was attended by both older and younger leaders. After deliberations, they decided to repudiate the treaty. Jabr returned to Baghdad to defend his position but to no avail. Rioting and demonstrations increased, and Jabr was forced to resign.

The new treaty was not the root cause of the uprising. It was the culmination of a struggle between the young, liberal leaders who wanted to participate in political activities and the older leaders who insisted on excluding them. This conflict continued after the treaty was rejected. The older politicians returned to power under Nūrī al-Saʿīd's leadership.

In 1952 another popular uprising flared, stirred by opposition leaders and carried out by students and extremists. The police were unable to control the mob, and the regent called on the army to maintain public order. The chief of the general staff governed the country under martial law for more than two months. Civilian rule was restored at the beginning of 1953, but there was no sign that the country's older leaders were prepared to share authority with their opponents.

Meanwhile, King Fayṣal II, who had come of age, began to exercise his formal powers, and the period of regency came to an end. It was hoped that 'Abd al-Ilāh would withdraw from active politics and allow the political forces of the country to create a new order. The former regent, who became the crown prince, continued to control political events from behind the scenes, however, and the struggle for power among the leaders continued with increasing intensity until the downfall of the monarchy in 1958.

In spite of political instability, Iraq achieved material progress during the 1950s, thanks to a new oil agreement that increased royalties and to the establishment of the

After coming of age, Fayṣal II constantly struggled for power with his uncle and former regent 'Abd al-Ilāh until the fall of the monarchy. AFP/ Getty Images

Development Board. The original oil agreement between the Iraqi government and the IPC had heretofore yielded relatively modest royalties, owing to certain technical limitations (such as the need for pipelines) and to war conditions. It was not until 1952 that construction of pipelines to Bāniyās was completed.

Some points of dispute between the government and the IPC were not entirely resolved. The nationalization of the oil industry in Iran and the announcement of the 1950 agreement between Saudi Arabia and Aramco (Arabian American Oil Company, later Saudi Aramco), on a half-and-half basis of payment, induced the Iraqi government and the IPC to negotiate a new agreement on the division of profits. Some opposition leaders demanded that the oil industry be nationalized, but the Iraqi government and the IPC, forestalling any serious move for nationalization, agreed to negotiate on the basis of the fifty-fifty formula, to the mutual advantage of Iraq and the company. The new agreement, signed in 1952, allowed Iraq to take part of its share of the profits in kind and to receive an increasing amount of royalties specifically agreed upon between the two parties. It was stated that Iraq would receive a set minimum amount of the proceeds in 1953 and all subsequent years.

In 1950 the government had created an independent Development Board, an agency immune from political pressures and responsible directly to the prime minister. The board had six executive members, three of whom had to be experts in some branch of the development program. The prime minister, as chairman, and the minister of finance were ex officio members. An amendment to the law increased membership by two and provided for a minister of development responsible directly to the head of the cabinet. These members were appointed by the cabinet, had equal voting rights, and were not permitted to hold any other official position. Two foreign members held positions as experts, and the Iraqi members were selected on merit and past experience. The board was composed of a council and ministry. Its staff was divided into technical sections and the ministry into a number of departments. The technical sections were for irrigation, flood control, water storage, drainage, transportation, and industrial and agricultural development. The board was financed from 70 percent of oil royalties and from loans and revenues from the board's own projects.

In 1950 the World Bank provided a loan for the Wadi Al-Tharthār flood-control project, and other flood-control plans were constructed. Extensive work on bridges and public buildings—including schools, hospitals, a new Parliament building, and a royal house—was started. This work, especially the work on dams and irrigation projects, was a long-term investment, and many short-term projects of more direct benefit to the population were neglected. Opposition leaders attacked the Development Board for the stress on long-term projects that they claimed benefited only the vested interests—landowners and tribal chiefs. In spite of criticism, the board maintained an independent status rarely enjoyed by any other government department. Nevertheless, the public remained unaware of the far-reaching effects of the projects undertaken, while the opposition attacked the board for squandering funds on contracts given to wealthy landlords and influential politicians.

THE REPUBLIC OF IRAQ

In spite of the country's material progress, the monarchy failed to win public support and, in particular, the confidence of the younger generation. Before the 1958 revolution, Iraq lacked an enlightened leadership capable of achieving progress and inspiring public confidence. The new generation offered such leadership, but the older leaders resisted and embarked on an unpopular foreign policy, including an alliance with Britain through participation in the Baghdad Pact and opposition to the establishment of the United Arab Republic (U.A.R.) by Egypt and Syria.

The 1958 Revolution and Its Aftermath

The failure of younger civilians to obtain power aroused the concern of some young military officers who, required by military discipline to take no part in politics, called themselves the Free Officers and began to organize in small groups and to lay down revolutionary plans. The number of Free Officers was relatively small, but there was a considerably larger group of sympathizers. The officers worked in cells, and the identities of the participants were kept secret. Only the Central Organization, which supplied the movement's leadership, was known to all the Free Officers. The Central Organization was composed of 14 officers, headed by 'Abd al-Karīm Qāsim, the group's highest-ranking member.

Of the several plots proposed, that laid down by Qāsim and his close collaborator 'Abd al-Salām 'Ārif proved the most appropriate. The general staff issued an order to the brigade in which 'Ārif served to proceed to Jordan in July 1958 to reinforce Jordanian forces against alleged threats by Israel. Brigadier Qāsim, in command of another brigade, was to protect the troops going to Jordan. He and 'Ārif agreed that, as the brigade proceeding to Jordan passed through Baghdad, it would capture the city.

On July 14 the revolutionary forces captured the capital, declared the downfall of the monarchy, and proclaimed a republic. The leading members of the royal house, including the king and the crown prince, were executed, and Nūrī al-Saʿīd was killed. Qāsim, head of the revolutionary force, formed a cabinet, over which he presided, and appointed himself commander of the national forces. He also assumed the portfolio of defense minister and appointed ʿĀrif minister of the interior and deputy commander of the national forces. A Council of Sovereignty, composed of three persons, was to act as head of state.

A provisional constitution declared that Iraq formed an integral part "of the Arab nation" and that "Arabs and Kurds are considered partners in this homeland." Iraq was declared a republic and Islam the religion of the state; all executive and legislative powers were entrusted to the Sovereignty Council and the cabinet. It soon became clear, however, that power rested in Qāsim's hands, supported by the army.

Conflicts among the officers developed, first between Qāsim and ʿĀrif and then between Qāsim and his supporters. ʿĀrif championed the pan-Arab cause and advocated Iraq's union with the U.A.R. Qāsim rallied the forces against Arab unity—Kurds, communists, and others—and stressed Iraq's own identity and internal unity. ʿĀrif was dropped from power in October, but in 1959 Qāsim's power was threatened by other factions. He tried to divert public attention to foreign affairs by advancing Iraq's claim to Kuwait's sovereignty in June 1961. This brought him into conflict not only with Britain and Kuwait but also with the other Arab countries. He opened negotiations with the Iraq Petroleum Company to increase Iraq's share of the royalties, but his extreme demands caused negotiations to break down in 1961. Public Law 80 was enacted to prohibit the granting of concessions to any foreign company and to transfer control over all matters connected with oil to the Iraq National Oil Company (INOC).

By 1963 Qāsim was isolated both internally and externally. He had survived several assassination attempts (a participant in one such attack was young Ṣaddām Ḥussein), and the only great power with which he remained friendly was the Soviet Union. When one faction of the army, in cooperation with one Arab nationalist group—the Iraqi regional branch of the Arab Socialist Ba'th ("Revivalist" or "Renaissance") Party—started a rebellion in February 1963, the regime suddenly collapsed, and Qāsim was executed.

'Abd al-Karīm Qāsim

(b. 1914, Baghdad, Iraq—d. Feb. 9, 1963, Baghdad)

'Abd al-Karīm Qāsim was an army officer who participated in the overthrow the Iraqi monarchy in 1958 and became head of the newly formed Republic of Iraq. Qāsim attended the Iraqi military academy and advanced steadily through the ranks until by 1955 he had become a high-ranking officer. Like many Iraqis, he disliked the socially conservative and pro-Western policies of the monarchy. By 1957 Qāsim had assumed leadership of the several opposition groups that had formed in the army. On July 14, 1958, Qāsim and his followers used troop movements planned by the government as an opportunity to seize military control of Baghdad and overthrow the monarchy. Qāsim became prime minister and assumed direction of a new republic.

The major issue facing Qāsim was that of Arab unity. The union of Egypt and Syria into the United Arab Republic (U.A.R.) early in 1958 had aroused immense enthusiasm in the Arab world. In spite of strong Pan-Arab sentiment in Iraq, Qāsim was determined to achieve internal stability before considering any kind of federation with the U.A.R. In turn the Egyptian president, Gamal Abdel Nasser, came to resent Qāsim's rule and tried to bring about its downfall. 'Abd al-Salām 'Ārif, a close supporter of Qāsim but also an ardent Nasserist, toured Iraq, praising Nasser. In March 1959 Pan-Arab opponents of Qāsim launched an open rebellion in Mosul. The bulk of the army remained loyal, so the uprising was crushed with little difficulty. Qāsim removed some 200 army officers of whose loyalty he could not be certain. Among civilians he was forced to rely for support mostly upon communists, who were eager for a chance to strike at their right-wing opponents, the Pan-Arabs, and now pushed for a larger voice in the determination of government policy. Qāsim resisted their demands, and several months later purged communist elements from the police and the army.

Qāsim's support as prime minister steadily narrowed. By 1960 he had suspended organized political activity and repressed both right- and left-wing civilian and military elements when it seemed that they might compete with his authority. His rule was supported only by the army, but in the spring of 1961 a rebellion broke out among the Kurds—an ethnic group acutely conscious of its cultural differences from the Arabs and to which Qāsim had neglected to fulfill a promise for a measure of autonomy within the Iraqi state. This Kurdish revolt undermined even Qāsim's military support, as much of the army became tied down in a seemingly endless and fruitless attempt to put down the rebellion. This situation, along with the discontent produced by repeated military purges, drew a number of officers into open resistance to the Qāsim regime. 'Ārif led dissident army elements in a coup in February 1963, which overthrew the government and killed Qāsim himself.

Recurrence of Military Coups, 1963–68

The military faction that brought about the collapse of the Qāsim regime preferred to remain behind the scenes rather than assume direct responsibility. The Ba'th Party, a group of young activists who advocated Arab nationalism and socialism, was entrusted with power. Ba'th leaders invited 'Abd al-Salām 'Ārif to assume the presidency. A National Council for Revolutionary Command (NCRC), composed of civilian and military leaders, was established to assume legislative and executive powers. The premiership was entrusted to Col. Aḥmad Ḥasan al-Bakr, a Ba'thist officer.

Some of the Ba'th leaders wanted to carry out Ba'th socialist ideas, but others advised more caution. A compromise was finally reached in which the party's goals—Arab unity, freedom, and socialism—were reaffirmed in principle, but it was decided to adopt a transitional program. Industrialization and economic development were stressed, and the role of the middle class was recognized. The dissension among Ba'th leaders, however, soon led to the collapse of the regime. President 'Ārif, whose powers initially had been restricted by the Ba'th leaders, rallied the military forces to his side. In November 1963 he placed the leaders of the Ba'th Party under arrest and took control, becoming, in both fact and name, the real ruler of the country. In May 1964 a new provisional constitution was promulgated in which the principles of Arab unity and socialism were adopted, and in July the banks and a number of the country's industries were nationalized.

The idea of Arab socialism attracted only a small group in Iraq, and 'Ārif began to discover its unfavourable effects on the country. 'Ārif himself had never been a believer in socialism, but he had adopted it under the influence of Egypt. The adverse influence of nationalization gave him an excuse to replace the group that supported socialism with others who would pay attention to the reality of Iraq's economic conditions. Nor had 'Ārif been happy with the group of officers who had elevated him to power. He began to prepare the way to entrusting power to civilian hands willing to be guided by him as chief executive.

In September 1965 'Ārif invited 'Abd al-Raḥman al-Bazzāz, a distinguished lawyer, diplomat, and writer on Arab nationalism, to form a new government. Al-Bazzāz did not feel that he should abolish Arab socialism, but he offered to increase production and create a balance between the public and private sectors.

'Ārif died suddenly in a helicopter crash in April 1966. Even before his death, Prime Minister al-Bazzāz, known for his opposition to military interference in politics, had begun to talk about the need to hold elections for a representative assembly. Military officers pressured the new president, 'Abd al-Raḥman 'Ārif, elder brother of the late president, to remove al-Bazzāz, and the cabinet resigned in August 1966. Power remained in military hands, but factionalism in the army was accentuated and leadership frequently changed. The Arab defeat in the June (Six-Day) War of 1967, in which Iraq took only a nominal role, led to intense unrest within the country and within the party. The Ba'th, joined by other opposition leaders, called for the formation of a coalition government and general elections for a National Assembly. President 'Ārif paid no attention to their demands.

Iraqi Foreign Policy, 1958–68

Following the 1958 revolution, President Qāsim steered his country's foreign policy gradually away from the sphere of Western influence—and close ties with the United Kingdom—toward closer relations with the Soviet Union. In 1959 Iraq officially left the pro-Western Baghdad Pact, but, though the Qāsim government came to depend on Soviet weapons and received some economic aid, it retained lively commercial ties with the West. Further, because Qāsim recruited among the Iraqi Communist Party for support and because he moved far closer to the Soviet Union diplomatically, the United States grew to see in him a would-be communist. However, in spite of a growing dispute with the Western oil companies over their investments in Iraq (stemming from Qāsim's demand of a greater share of the proceeds) and steps by the government that limited oil company activities in Iraq, Qāsim carefully refrained from nationalizing Iraq's oil industry.

Also, fearing Egyptian domination, as had happened in the Syrian province of the U.A.R., Qāsim rejected the courtship of Egyptian Pres. Gamal Abdel Nasser and refused a merger with Egypt. This led the two Free Officers' regimes—as the Egyptian regime was also termed—into a conflict that greatly embarrassed the Soviet Union and occasionally forced it to take sides.

This also strongly influenced Qāsim's approach to Israel. Although he paid lip service to anti-Zionist sentiments in Iraq, there was no way that he and Nasser could collaborate against Israel, and tension with the Hāshimite monarchy of Jordan made it impossible for him to send an expeditionary force to Jordan, even had he wanted to do so. On the Israeli side this fact was fully appreciated at the time. Relations with pro-Western Iran were tense also, but the two countries avoided a direct military confrontation.

Qāsim's relations with most of the Arab world worsened after Iraq left the Arab League in 1961 in protest against the organization's support for Kuwait's independence. Iraq had continued to press its claims to Kuwaiti territory in the 1940s and '50s (largely over the islands of Būbiyān and Warbah), but not until the Qāsim regime did it forward a serious claim of overall sovereignty. In 1963, after Qāsim's demise, Kuwait came to an agreement with Aḥmad Ḥasan al-Bakr—who was then Iraq's prime minister—confirming Kuwait's independence and resolving all border issues. Once again the agreement failed to be ratified, however, this time by Iraq's president, 'Abd al-Salām 'Ārif.

The Ba'th-'Ārif regime (February–November 1963) had little time for foreign policy formulation, as the various party factions were far too busy fighting one another. Having killed thousands of communists and their supporters, however, the Ba'th regime completely alienated the Soviet Union, and Soviet weapons shipments stopped. The regime also alienated Egypt by rejecting the U.A.R.

merger. Of all the Arab countries, only relations with Syria, again independent and now also under Ba'th rule, remained cordial.

During the regimes of the 'Ārif brothers (1963–68), Iraq remained essentially within the Soviet sphere of influence, but in early 1967 there were signs of a limited rapprochement with the West. Iraq's Arab relations improved greatly, albeit at the expense of Iraqi independence. 'Abd al-Salām 'Ārif reversed the country's policy toward Nasser's government in Egypt, in effect turning Iraq into an Egyptian satellite. Although it was Nasser who now rejected Iraq's request for unification, relations between the two countries became extremely close. 'Abd al-Salām's policy toward Israel mimicked that of Egypt, and, when tensions along the Israeli-Egyptian border grew to the dangerous proportions that led to the June War of 1967, the Iraqi leader dispatched an armoured brigade to Jordan. Events moved too fast, however, and most of the brigade was destroyed by the Israeli air force before it could reach the front line.

The Revolution of 1968

After 'Abd al-Salām 'Ārif took control in 1963, the Ba'th Party was forced underground and began to make sweeping changes in its leadership and strategy in order to recapture power. Al-Bakr became secretary of the Regional Leadership (RL) of the Ba'th Party in 1964. He was assisted in reorganizing the party by Ṣaddām Ḥussein, who proved to be instrumental in rallying civilian Ba'thist support for al-Bakr. A premature attempt to seize power in September 1964 led to the imprisonment of the principal Ba'th leaders, including al-Bakr and Ṣaddām. In 1965 al-Bakr was released because of illness, and in 1966 Ṣaddām escaped.

In July 1968 the government was overthrown by the army, with some assistance from civilian party activists. The reasons given were the corruption of the ʿĀrif regime, Kurdish disturbances in the north, the government's failure to adequately support other Arab countries in the June War of 1967, and ʿĀrif's subservience to Nasser's Egypt. Except for the charge of corruption (ʿĀrif had no bank accounts abroad and had little property inside Iraq), the charges were valid but were only circumstantial. The root causes went much deeper. The ʿĀrif regime, because it had not held popular elections, had failed to attain legitimacy. Barring that, it failed even to attempt to build a party structure or mobilize mass support. Instead, it depended completely on military support, which since 1936 had been inconsistent and capricious. Finally, ʿAbd al-Raḥmān ʿĀrif was anything but an inspiring leader. When the Baʿth Party persuaded a few officers in key positions to abandon the regime, the fate of the ʿĀrif government was sealed.

Four officers agreed to cooperate with the Baʿth Party. These were Col. ʿAbd al-Razzāq al-Nāyif, head of military intelligence; Col. Ibrāhīm ʿAbd al-Raḥman al-Dāʾūd, chief of the Republican Guard; Col. Saʿdūn Ghaydān; and Col. Hammād Shihāb. The first two agreed to cooperate on condition that al-Nāyif be the new premier and al-Dāʾūd the minister of defense. Shihāb agreed to help on the condition that ʿĀrif not be harmed. The Baʿth Party accepted this arrangement as a means to achieve power but intended to bridle the officers at the earliest-possible moment, having little confidence in their loyalty.

On the morning of July 17, President ʿĀrif's palace was stormed by Baʿthist officers led by al-Bakr. ʿĀrif immediately surrendered and agreed to leave the country. He went to London and then to Istanbul, where he lived in modest obscurity, before returning to Iraq some 20 years later.

The first act of the new regime was to establish the Revolutionary Command Council (RCC), which assumed supreme authority. The RCC elected al-Bakr president of the republic, and he invited al-Nāyif to form a cabinet. Al-Bakr was not interested in administrative details, and, as he grew older and his health deteriorated, he began to depend more heavily on Ṣaddām to carry out the business of government.

Almost immediately a struggle for power arose between the Baʿth and the Nāyif-Dāʾūd group, ostensibly over socialism and foreign policy but in fact over which of the two groups was to control the regime. On July 30 al-Nāyif was arrested by Ṣaddām and a group of armed party activists and officers. It was agreed that al-Nāyif's life would be spared if he left the country, and he was sent to Morocco as ambassador, whereas al-Dāʾūd, who was then on a mission to Jordan, was instructed to remain there.

This second bloodless coup, which did not cause any disturbances in Iraq, cleared the way for the Baʿth Party to control the regime. Al-Bakr assumed the premiership in addition to the presidency and the chairmanship of the RCC. Most cabinet posts were given to Baʿth leaders. Sympathizers of the Nāyif-Dāʾūd group were removed, and a number of civil servants considered unfriendly to the regime were retired or relieved of duty. Most important, over the next few weeks some 2,000 to 3,000 army and air force officers were forced to retire, being regarded as a security risk by the ruling party. Most were supporters of Nasser, who, in spite of the best efforts of the regime, maintained a following within the military until his death in 1970.

The Interim Constitution was issued in September 1968. It provided for an essentially presidential system composed of the RCC, the cabinet, and the National Assembly. Until the National Assembly was called, the RCC exercised both executive and legislative powers and, occasionally, judicial powers as well. After November 1969, with few exceptions, RCC members were elected or nominated out of the RL. In this way the civilian party—now in reality led by Vice President Ṣaddām Ḥussein—was able to eventually remove all army officers from power and maintain control. In the state as a whole, the Baʿth Party, already highly organized, began to infiltrate and influence almost all national organizations.

Disturbances in the Kurdish area and several attempts to overthrow the regime kept the Baʿth leaders preoccupied and prevented them from launching planned social and economic programs. The attempts to overthrow the regime were suppressed without difficulty, but the Kurdish problem proved more complicated.

Even before the Baʿth Party achieved power, the Kurdish question had been discussed in several meetings of the Baʿth Party leadership. However, in late 1968 fighting between the Kurds and the Iraqi army began once again and escalated to full-scale warfare. With military aid provided by Iran, the Kurds were able to pose a serious threat to the Baʿth regime. By early 1970 negotiations between the Baʿth leaders, with Ṣaddām as chief government negotiator, the Kurdish leader Muṣṭafā al-Barzānī, and other leaders of the Kurdish Democratic Party (KDP) were under way. The government agreed to officially recognize the Kurds as a "national" group entitled to a form of autonomous status called self-rule. This would eventually lead to the establishment of a provincial administrative council and an assembly to deal with Kurdish affairs. The agreement was proclaimed in the Manifesto of March 1970, to go into effect in March 1974, following a census to determine the frontiers of the area in which the Kurds formed the majority of the population.

In April 1972 Iraq and the Soviet Union signed a treaty in which the two countries agreed to cooperate in political, economic, and military affairs. The Soviet Union also agreed to supply Iraq with arms.

To strengthen the Ba'th regime, two important steps were taken. First, the conflict with the Iraqi Communist Party (ICP), which had arisen after the revolution of 1958 and had led to the death of thousands of communists under Ba'th rule, was reconciled. Second, the National Progressive Front was established to provide legitimacy to the regime by enlisting the support of other political parties. Since the March Manifesto had established a basis for settling the Kurdish problem, Kurdish political parties were willing to participate in the National Progressive Front (NPF). The ICP had also shown interest. A Charter for National Action, prepared by the Ba'th Party, was published in the press for public discussion and became the basis for cooperation with the ICP and other parties.

In March 1972 Ba'thist and ICP leaders met to discuss the content of the charter and express their views about basic principles such as socialism, democracy, and economic development. A statute was drawn up expressing the principles agreed on as the basis for cooperation among the parties of the NPF. It also provided for a 16-member central executive committee, called the High Committee, and a secretariat. The NPF officially came into existence in 1973.

In 1973–74 negotiations with al-Barzānī and the KDP to implement the March Manifesto failed. The census promised in the March Manifesto had not been taken, and al-Barzānī and the KDP refused to accept the Ba'thist determination of the borders of the Kurdish area, which excluded the oil-rich Karkūk province. Nevertheless, in March 1974 the Ba'th regime proceeded to implement its own plan for self-rule, establishing a provincial council and an assembly in cooperation with Kurdish leaders who were opposed to al-Barzānī's militant approach. Iraq also set up the Kurdish Autonomous Region in the three predominantly Kurdish governorates of Arbīl, Dahūk, and Al-Sulaymāniyyah.

The Kurdish war started in March 1974. Al-Barzānī's decision to go to war with the Ba'th government seems to have been made with the support of the shah of Iran, who sought to pressure Iraq to alter the water frontier in the Shatt al-Arab to the thalweg, or the deepest point of the river. (Under the terms of the 1937 treaty, the boundary was set at the low-water mark on the Iranian side, giving Iraq control of the shipping channel.) Soon after the conflict broke out, however, an agreement between Iran and Iraq caused Iran to suspend support for the Kurds and ended the Kurdish war. Al-Barzānī's forces and political supporters were given a few days to withdraw into Iran, and the Iraqi government took full control of Iraqi Kurdistan.

Relations between the Ba'th regime and the ICP deteriorated after 1975. Ba'th policies were openly criticized in the communist press. Many communists were arrested, and by 1979 most of the principal ICP leaders were either in prison or had left Iraq. The absence of communist representation deprived the NPF of an opposition party that was willing to voice dissent on fundamental issues.

Foreign Policy 1968–80

The Ba'th Party came to power, to a large extent, on the waves of deep popular frustration that followed the Arab defeat by Israel in the June War. The party soon became, rhetorically, the most extreme anti-Israeli regime in the Arab world, promising to quickly conduct a successful war to wrest Palestine from Israeli control. The Ba'th retained, and even reinforced, a large and expensive expeditionary force in Jordan, yet it vitiated its own agenda by alienating virtually every regime in the Arab world. The party was extremely unpopular inside Iraq because of its disastrous experience in 1963, and both the public and the military were still to a large extent under the influence of Nasser. The party believed that, by besmirching the Egyptian leader, it could gain public support. It called on Nasser to resign for having failed the Arab world in the war and for having rejected Iraq's demand to launch another, immediate attack. Relations with Ba'thist Syria also became tense. The oil monarchies of the Persian Gulf were wary of Ba'th social, national, and anti-Western radicalism, fearing Iraq might inspire revolutionary activities in their countries, and, indeed, the Ba'th regime called for Ba'th-style revolutions throughout the Arab world.

Beginning in the spring of 1969, relations with the Iranian monarchy also deteriorated over control of the Shatt al-Arab and over Iranian support for Iraq's Kurdish rebels. Relations remained cordial, though reserved, only with Jordan, because Iraq needed Jordanian cooperation in order to keep Iraqi forces in that country. During a clash between the Jordanian government and the Palestine Liberation Organization in September 1970, the Iraqi government decided to avoid a confrontation with Jordanian troops (in spite of earlier promises to aid the Palestinians) and withdrew its forces east, into the Jordanian desert. This won them harsh criticism from the Palestinians and from Arab radicals in general. However, it could not save their relations with Jordan, which during the next few years reached a nadir.

Beginning in 1974–75, under the direction of Ṣaddām, Iraq's relations with its neighbours started to improve. The young vice president realized that the country's near total isolation was threatening the regime's hold on power. The crucial turnaround took place in 1975 when Iraq and Iran signed the Algiers Agreement, in which Iraq agreed to move the maritime boundary between the two countries to the thalweg—conditioned on Iran's withdrawal of support for the Iraqi Kurds. This was followed by improved relations with most gulf states, and in 1975 Egypt's new president, Anwar el-Sādāt, and the Sudan's president, Gaafar Mohamed el-Nimeiri, each visited Baghdad. In the years that followed, relations with Jordan and Turkey also improved dramatically.

Besides Israel, the only close neighbour with which Iraq did not experience improved relations was Syria. Tension between the two Ba'thist regimes increased throughout the 1970s, and both sought to undermine the other. In 1976, as part of a dispute over oil-transfer revenues, Iraq stopped shipping oil through Syrian pipelines, opting rather to use a newer pipeline across Turkey. That this ongoing dispute conflicted with the Ba'thist's pan-Arab rhetoric apparently was of little importance: the main task for Ṣaddām was to keep the Ba'th Party in power in Baghdad, and the destabilizing influence of the Syrian branch of the party was something he could not afford. Only by denigrating the Syrian regime—as Ṣaddām frequently did—by accusing it of betraying the party's ideals and of colluding with Israel could he clearly signal members of his own branch of the party that involvement with Syria would lead to charges of treason.

Throughout the 1970s, while Iraq's anti-Israeli rhetoric reached a crescendo, the Ba'th regime in Baghdad also began to play down its commitment to any immediate war against Israel. As Ṣaddām explained it to his domestic audience, the Arabs were not ready for such a war, because there was a need to first achieve strategic superiority over the Jewish state. Ṣaddām's vision was that Iraq first would concentrate exclusively on economic, technological, and military growth, turning itself into a "fortress." Only when Iraq was ready would it turn outside, "radiating" its influence to the Arab world. Only then, under Iraq's leadership, would the Arabs be ready to confront Israel. In fact, there was a notable leap in almost every sector of Iraq's economy and in military expansion during the late 1970s. This military development also included Iraq's first meaningful investment in nuclear and biological weapons research.

Economic Development to 1980

Perhaps the greatest assets of the Ba'th regime were the ambitious plans for reconstruction and development laid down by its leaders. The struggle for power during 1958–68 had left little time for constructive work, and the Ba'th Party sought not only to transform the economic system from free enterprise to collectivism but also to assert the country's economic independence. The immediate objectives were to increase production and to raise the standard of living, but the ultimate objective was to establish a socialist society in which all citizens would enjoy the benefits of progress and prosperity. On the other hand, the regime's socioeconomic program was an effective way of controlling the population. Critics of the regime have defined this system as combining "intimidation and enticement" (*al-tarhīb wa al-targhīb*): along with building a huge and extremely brutal internal-security apparatus, the regime expended the country's vast oil revenues to create an extensive welfare system and to extend roads, electric grids, and water-purification systems to much of the countryside.

The five-year economic plans of 1965–70 and 1971–75 concentrated on raising the level of production in both agriculture and industry and aimed at reducing dependence on oil revenues as the primary source for development. But agriculture lagged far behind target goals, and industrial development was slow. The five-year plan of 1976–80, formulated in the years after Iraq's oil revenues had suddenly quadrupled, was far more ambitious. Development goals in virtually every category were intended to increase, reaching two and even three times the levels of previous plans. Altogether the allocation for development compared with previous plans increased more than 10-fold, eventually reaching some one-third of the general budget. Ideologically, the regime now sought to legitimize itself through economic development rather than through extremist revolutionary rhetoric, as it had done previously. In practice, however, the funds may have been available to meet these goals, but the country's inadequate infrastructure made implementation unachievable. Also, though many large industrial plants were constructed, production was inefficient, and Iraqi state products could compete on the world markets only in situations where Iraq had a meaningful advantage, such as in products that directly exploited the country's petroleum surplus.

Ba'th leaders considered nationalizing the oil industry their greatest achievement. Between 1969 and 1972 several agreements with foreign powers—the Soviet Union and others—were concluded to provide the Iraq National Oil Company (INOC) with the capital and technical skills to exploit the oil fields. In 1972 operation started at the highly productive North Rumaylah field, and an Iraqi Oil Tankers Company was established to deliver oil to several foreign countries. Also in 1972 the Iraq Petroleum Company (IPC) was nationalized (with compensation), and a national company, the Iraqi Company for Oil Operations, was established to operate the fields. In 1973, when the Yom Kippur War broke out, Iraq nationalized American and Dutch companies, and in 1975 it nationalized the remaining foreign interests in the Basra Petroleum Company.

The initial step in agrarian reform had been taken with the Agrarian Reform Law of 1958, which provided for distributing to peasants lands in excess of a certain maximum ownership. A decade later less than half of the land had been distributed. In 1969 a revised Agrarian Reform Law relieved the peasants from payments for their land by abolishing compensation to landowners, and a year later a new Agrarian Reform Law was designed to improve the conditions of the peasantry, increase agricultural production, and correlate development in rural and urban areas. The results were disappointing, however, because of the difficulty officials had in persuading the peasants to stay on their farms and because of their inability to improve the quality of agricultural production. The Ba'th regime also completed work on irrigation projects that had already been under way and began new projects in areas where water was likely to be scarce in the summer. In the five-year plan of 1976–80, funds were allocated for completion of dams on the Euphrates, Tigris, Diyālā, and upper Zab rivers and Lake al-Tharthār.

The Ba'th regime allocated funds to finish dam work on rivers such as the Tigris. Karim Sahib/AFP/Getty Images

Recognizing that a rapid transition to full socialism was neither possible nor in the country's best interest, the Ba'th provided for a sector (albeit a small one) for private investors, and a third, mixed sector was created in which private and public enterprises could cooperate. This three-tier economy, however, provided fertile ground for official corruption, and senior government officials received illicit commissions for approving deals between the public and private sectors.

Iraq Under Ṣaddām Ḥussein

From the early 1970s Ṣaddām was widely recognized as the power behind President al-Bakr, who after 1977 was little more than a figurehead. Ṣaddām reached this position through his leadership of the internal security apparatus, a post that most senior Ba'thist figures had been too squeamish to fill. Ṣaddām, however, had drawn hard lessons from the party's failure in 1963 and resolved that no dissent should be allowed in party ranks, no opposition outside the party should be tolerated, and ideological commitment to party ideals alone was insufficient to guarantee the loyalty of internal security officers. Kinship bonds were, to him, much more promising. President al-Bakr concurred on that issue, and soon after the Ba'th takeover al-Bakr appointed his young relative (both al-Bakr and Ṣaddām belonged to the tribe of Āl Bū Nāṣir) to the powerful posts of deputy chairman of the RCC, deputy secretary-general of the RL, and vice president. Al-Bakr also allowed Ṣaddām to form the Presidential Guard, mostly from members of the Āl Bū Nāṣir and allied Sunni tribes. Between 1968 and the mid-1970s Ṣaddām became the unchallenged leader of internal security. After he jailed, executed, or assassinated the regime's opponents, he turned against his own opponents inside the ruling party, using the same tools and methods: a plethora of ubiquitous and ruthless internal security organs loyal to him personally.

It was virtually taken for granted that when al-Bakr relinquished the presidency, Ṣaddām would succeed him. Nevertheless, his succession was not carried out without complications. Perhaps the two most important complicating factors were Egyptian President Sādāt's decision to make peace with Israel and Syrian Pres. Ḥāfiẓ al-Assad's bid for economic and political union with Iraq. These two events were not unrelated. In spite of ongoing tensions between the two branches of the Baʿth Party, Arab unity had been a long-standing party goal in both Syria and Iraq. Assad, however, was prompted to call for union with Iraq only after Egypt's rapprochement with Israel in 1977. While President al-Bakr hesitated, Ṣaddām strongly resisted this move. After Egypt and Israel signed the Camp David Accords in 1978, however, there was no way he could avoid the issue.

The initial negotiations showed great promise. Talks in October 1978 led to the signing of a "charter for joint national action," which declared the two countries' intent to establish military unity. By 1979 it was clear that the eventual aim was full political union. Iraq and Syria also cooperated with other Arab leaders in taking a firm stand against Sādāt. By March 1979, however, when Sādāt signed a peace treaty with Israel, negotiations for a Syro-Iraqi union had slowed. The main stumbling block was the question of whether the leadership of the unified state would be primarily Syrian or Iraqi.

Relations between the two countries deteriorated, and by that time Ṣaddām had an additional reason for avoiding ties with Damascus: Iran's Islamic revolution had installed a regime that was clearly anti-Iraqi and had close ties with Syria. The Iraqi regime also saw a vague religious threat, inasmuch as many among Syria's ruling elite adhered to a branch of Shīʿism (the ʿAlawī sect) that was faintly related to that practiced in revolutionary Iran. Given Iraq's large—and for the most part disfranchised—Shīʿite population, Baghdad perceived relations between Syria and Iran as an unprecedented threat.

On July 16, 1979, the eve of the anniversary of the revolution of 1968, al-Bakr officially announced his resignation. There is little doubt that Ṣaddām forced him to resign. Al-Bakr was placed under de facto house arrest and died in 1982. Ṣaddām immediately succeeded him as president, chairman of the RCC, secretary-general of the RL, and commander in chief of the armed forces.

Less than two weeks after Ṣaddām claimed leadership, it was announced that a plot to overthrow the government had been uncovered. This announcement had been preceded some days earlier by the arrest of Muḥyī ʿAbd al-Ḥusayn al-Mashhadī, the secretary of the RCC (and, not coincidentally, a Shīʿite). Mashhadī made a public confession that was, in all likelihood, coerced. He stated that he and other Baʿth leaders, including four other members of the RCC, in collaboration with the Syrian government, had conspired to overthrow the regime. It is doubtful such a conspiracy existed, and it is unclear why those individuals were eliminated—all had been, at one time or another, protégés of Ṣaddām. However, they had opposed al-Bakr's resignation and Ṣaddām's ascendancy to the presidency. Thus, Ṣaddām had finally managed to abort rapprochement between Iraq and Syria and, at the same time, send a message to all party members that the new president would not tolerate even the slightest dissent. A special court was set up, and 22 other senior officials were tried and executed; a number of others were sentenced to prison terms.

Syria denied complicity in any plot, but Ṣaddām accused it of planning acts of sabotage and murder, and the Syrian ambassador and his staff were expelled. The Syrians reciprocated. With the de facto termination of diplomatic ties, economic relations between the two Baʿthist regimes started to deteriorate. In April 1982, at the height of its war with Iran, Iraq needed additional maritime outlets. Syria responded by closing its border with Iraq—ostensibly to prevent Iraqi arms smuggling—and shutting down the Iraqi-Syrian oil pipeline. A few days later Syria officially severed diplomatic relations with Iraq.

The Iran-Iraq War

Relations with Iran had grown increasingly strained after the shah was overthrown in 1979. Iraq recognized Iran's new Shīʿite Islamic government, but the Iranian leaders would have nothing to do with the Baʿth regime, which they denounced as secular. Ruhollah Khomeini, the spiritual leader of the Iranian revolution, proclaimed his policy of "exporting the revolution," and Iraq was high on the list of countries whose governments were to be overthrown and replaced by a replica of the Islamic regime in Iran. In addition, Iran still occupied three small pieces of territory along the Iran-Iraq border that were supposed to be returned to Iraq under the treaty of 1975.

The Baʿth government was highly sensitive to the Islamic threat, not merely because it was a secular regime but because the ruling elite, in spite of some earnest efforts at enfranchisement, consisted mainly of Sunni Arabs. By the late 1970s the Shīʿites were an overall majority in the Baʿth Party, but members of that sect were a minority in the party's middle and upper levels. In the late

1980s Shīʿites still constituted only about one-fifth of all army general officers, and Shīʿite representation in the upper echelons of the internal security services was even lower. On the whole, Shīʿites remained aloof from the regime. This estrangement was attributable in large part to the socioeconomic gap between Sunnis and Shīʿites—the vast majority of Shīʿites being poor—but it was also a result of the regime's desire to control fully every walk of life. This included persistent attempts to control Shīʿite religious life—including education in madrasahs (religious colleges)—a situation objectionable to traditional Shīʿites and to Iraq's influential Shīʿite clergy, who maintained close ties with colleagues in Iran.

As long as the secular, Westernized shah ruled over Iran, traditional Iraqi Shīʿites remained politically quiescent. When Khomeini came to power in February 1979, however, his example inspired many Shīʿites in Iraq to engage in greater political activism. Mass pro-Khomeini demonstrations and guerrilla activity became regular occurrences. The man who encouraged these activities, and in whom many saw an Iraqi Khomeini, was the young and charismatic Ayatollah Muḥammad Bāqir al-Ṣadr. The regime cracked down on the Shīʿite movement with great ferocity, and hundreds were executed, some 10,000 were imprisoned, and tens of thousands were driven across the border into Iran. In April 1980 Ṣaddām ordered the execution of al-Ṣadr and his sister; by July demonstrations had ceased, and guerrilla activity had come to a virtual halt.

Still, the Baʿth regime feared that as long as Khomeini was in power, his Islamic revolution could serve as a source of inspiration for Shīʿite revolutionaries in Iraq. Further, Ṣaddām saw an assassination attempt against Ṭāriq ʿAzīz, the foreign minister and the president's close associate, by a Shīʿite activist as an insult directed against him personally. Under normal circumstances such developments would likely never have led to war, but Khomeini had isolated himself from the international community and had crippled his own armed forces through extensive purges of the shah's officers' corps. In addition, when Khomeini came to power in Iran, Iraq had a large, well-organized, and well-equipped military and a fast-growing economy. No less important, it enjoyed friendly relations with most of its neighbours, and all its armed forces had since been recalled to within its own borders.

It was those conditions that convinced Ṣaddām he could win a blitz war against the less-organized and internationally isolated Iran, in spite of the latter's greater size and superior natural and human resources. In doing this, the Iraqi leader's likely goals were to remove Khomeini from power and replace his regime with one more friendly to Iraq, demarcate the border (particularly along the Shatt al-Arab) in Iraq's favour, secure autonomy for Khūzestān (an oil-rich region in southwestern Iran inhabited largely by ethnic Arabs) under some Iraqi tutelage, and give Iraq hegemonic power in the Persian Gulf.

Beginning in 1979, border clashes began to occur frequently, and Ṣaddām announced in September 1980 that he was abrogating the 1975 agreements because they had been violated by Iran. Within days, Iraqi forces invaded Iran. At the same time, Iraq bombed Iranian air bases and other strategic targets. In the week following the invasion, the UN Security Council called for a cease-fire and appealed to Iran and Iraq to settle their dispute peacefully. The Iraqi president replied, saying that Iraq would accept a cease-fire provided Iran did as well. Iran's response, however, was negative. The war thus continued and in succeeding years was extended to the gulf area. It has been aptly called the Gulf War. (The hostilities of 1991 and 2003 have also been called gulf wars.)

The Iraqi advance into Iran was stopped in November 1980. There followed a stalemate that continued until September 1981, when Iran, which had rejected further attempts at mediation, began a series of successful offensives. By May 1982 the Iraqis had been driven from most of the captured territory. Iranian forces, having liberated the Iranian city of Khorramshahr and having lifted the siege of Ābādān, began to penetrate into Iraq's Al-Baṣrah province. During 1982–87 they threatened the city of Al-Baṣrah and occupied Majnūn Island and the Fāw (Fao) peninsula. In its unsuccessful attempts to liberate the Fāw peninsula during February–March 1986, Iraq suffered horrific casualties. The Iranian attacks on Al-Baṣrah were repulsed with heavy casualties on both sides. Iraq countered in the so-called tanker war by bombing Iranian oil terminals in the gulf, especially on Khārk Island.

In 1987 the military balance began to favour Iraq, which had raised an army of some one million and, while Iran remained largely isolated from the international community, had obtained state-of-the-art arms from France and the Soviet Union, including thousands of artillery pieces, tanks, and armoured personnel carriers and hundreds of combat aircraft. This arsenal (enormous for a country of some 18 million inhabitants) was bolstered by the addition of substantial quantities of chemical weapons, which the regime acquired or produced throughout the 1980s. At the same time, Iraq committed substantial resources in an attempt to develop or purchase other weapons of mass destruction (WMD), including biological and nuclear arms.

Relations with the United States, which had resumed in 1984, began to improve. In 1987 the United States agreed

In the late 1980s, Iraq dedicated substantial resources toward developing or acquiring weapons of mass destruction. Time & Life Pictures/Getty Images

to reflag 11 Kuwaiti tankers and escort them in international waters through the Strait of Hormuz. Britain and France also escorted tankers carrying their own flags. Although a U.S. destroyer was inadvertently attacked by an Iraqi bomber in May 1987, the United States supported Iraq, both diplomatically at the UN and militarily by providing information about Iranian military movements in the gulf area. In October 1987 and April 1988, U.S. forces attacked Iranian ships and oil platforms.

In July 1987 the UN Security Council had unanimously passed Resolution 598, urging Iraq and Iran to accept a cease-fire, withdraw their forces to internationally recognized boundaries, and settle their frontier disputes by negotiations held under UN auspices. Iraq agreed to abide by the terms if Iran reciprocated. Iran, however, demanded amendments condemning Iraq as the aggressor in the war (which would have held them liable for paying war reparations) and calling on all foreign navies to leave the gulf.

In the northeastern provinces Iranian forces, in cooperation with Iraqi Kurds, threatened the area from Karkūk to the Turkish border and penetrated to the Iraqi towns of Ḥājj ʿUmrān and Ḥalabjah. They met with stiff resistance in the north, however. Using chemical weapons, Iraqi forces inflicted heavy casualties on Kurdish civilians in and around Ḥalabjah in March 1988.

Military operations in the gulf resumed, and in April 1988 Iraq—this time using chemical weapons against the Iranian troops—recaptured the Fāw peninsula. Later it liberated the districts of Salamcha and Majnūn, and in July Iraqi forces once again penetrated deep into Iran. It became clear that Iran's military position in the gulf had become untenable, and it accepted Resolution 598, which came into force on Aug. 20, 1988. The war had been one of the most destructive conflicts of the late 20th century.

Hundreds of thousands had died, and large areas of western Iran and southeastern Iraq had been devastated.

When the foreign ministers of Iraq and Iran met for the first time in Geneva in August 1988 and later in 1989, there was no progress on how Resolution 598 was to be implemented. Iraq demanded the full exchange of prisoners as the first step, while Iran insisted that withdrawing Iraqi forces from Iran should precede the exchange of prisoners. (The last prisoners were not exchanged until 2003, as many Iraqi Shīʿites had been fearful of returning home.) The border dispute remained an ongoing point of friction between the two countries, even though Iran eventually allowed Iraq to make limited use of the Shatt al-Arab. In 1990 Iraq implied that it was ready to return to the 1975 agreement, but nothing came of the overture. Occasional diplomatic initiatives were afterward interlaced with small-scale military incidents along the border. Each country supported opposition groups that worked against the rival's government. Iraq sheltered the Mojāhedīn-e Khalq—an Iranian extremist group—and Iran lent support to various Iraqi Shīʿite groups. Guerrilla attacks and terrorist incidents were frequent in the years after the war.

Postwar Policies

Articles 47 to 56 of the interim Iraqi constitution provided for a legislative assembly, and—in an effort to garner popular support during the war—elections (the first in postrevolutionary Iraq) were held in June 1980. The new National Assembly convened 10 days later, and subsequent elections were held in 1984 and 1989. Regardless, the Assembly was vested with little power. Only those supporting the Baʿth revolution were allowed to stand for office, and in disputes between the Assembly and the RCC, the latter's decisions were final. Moreover, after Ṣaddām's rise to the presidency, the RCC itself had become increasingly irrelevant and eventually served as little more than a rubber stamp for the president's decisions. Within the Ba'th Party meaningful political debate did continue, but only on topics selected by the president, and all presidential decisions were final.

After the cease-fire, Iraq began a program of reconstruction, concentrating on the areas that had suffered most during the war, but the country had little ready cash. Iraq, now deeply in debt, continued to spend large sums on armaments, and inflation and unemployment soared. To relieve social pressures, the government made it easier for people to travel abroad, but few were able to take advantage of this policy. In addition, the government promised to open the political process by allowing multiparty elections and greater press freedoms. The draft constitution prepared in late 1989 was scrutinized by the RCC before it reached the National Assembly for approval and was about to be submitted to a public plebiscite when Iraq invaded Kuwait. Thereafter, the entire democratic plan was shelved.

To enhance Iraq's position in the Arab world, Ṣaddām had begun to negotiate a set of bilateral agreements with his neighbours. Early in 1989 he had concluded nonaggression pacts with Saudi Arabia and Bahrain. He also had established the Arab Cooperation Council with Jordan, Egypt, and Yemen to promote economic and cultural development.

Peace negotiations with Iran had not brought about a settlement, and Ṣaddām—in spite of Iraq's overwhelming military edge over Iran—continued to purchase weapons. Iraq's rearmament program included expensive programs to develop missiles and chemical, biological, and nuclear weapons. Criticism in the West of Iraq's record on human rights and the county's acquisition of sensitive military technology prompted Ṣaddām to make highly inflammatory speeches about the hostile Western attitude. In April 1990 he warned that if Israel ever again attacked Iraq (as that country had attacked and destroyed Iraq's Osiraq-Tammuz nuclear plant in 1981), he would retaliate with chemical weapons. This threat was later extended to include an attack by Israel on any Arab state, and Ṣaddām soon began to suggest that Iraq's eventual goal was to defeat Israel and capture Jerusalem. These declarations were the first indications that the Iraqi regime had wider territorial aspirations and portended the invasion of Kuwait less than a year later.

THE PERSIAN GULF WAR AND ITS CAUSES

Iraq characterized its war with Iran as a defensive action against the spread of the Islamic revolution not only to Iraq but to other gulf countries and to the wider Arab world and portrayed itself as "the eastern gate to the Arab homeland." Ṣaddām thus anticipated that the large war debt incurred by Iraq—much of it owed to the Persian Gulf monarchies—would be forgiven. He even expected the gulf countries to finance his reconstruction program, as the United States had financed the reconstruction of western Europe through the Marshall Plan. The Iraqi leadership was greatly angered when it saw support from the gulf Arab states dwindle after the war ended. Although Iraq's major financier, Kuwait, was willing to forgive the war debt—apparently for domestic considerations—it was reluctant to announce such an action to the world banking community. Tensions with Iraq grew further when several gulf states, including Kuwait, exceeded their oil-production quotas set by the Organization for Petroleum Exporting Countries (OPEC). This resulted in a sharp drop in world oil prices, costing Iraq substantial amounts of income. Suspecting that the increase in oil production was prompted by Western pressure, the Iraqi president criticized Kuwait and the United Arab Emirates for undermining his country's position, and he brought the matter to the attention of OPEC. The oil price for 1990 was raised, but suspicion and lack of cooperation still prevailed.

There were, however, other reasons for disagreement. Iraq was suspected by most gulf countries of having political ambitions, possibly including domination over some of the countries in the region. More specifically, Iraq held that it had historical claim to Kuwait's sovereignty dating to 1871, when the ruler of Kuwait was appointed subgovernor under Midhat Paşa. This claim had been pressed in 1961 during the Qāsim regime but had met with strong resistance by other Arab states and the broader international community. Yet Iraq's failure to ratify former agreements left room for further claims, and it sought additional border compromises, particularly control of the islands of Būbiyān and Warbah, the possession of which Iraq saw as crucial to defending its port at Umm Qaṣr.

Iraq's historic claims, the grievances that arose from the Iran-Iraq War, and Ṣaddām's desire to obtain strategic territory set the stage for confrontation, and these tensions were exacerbated when Iraq accused Kuwait of drilling horizontally into Iraq's Al-Rumaylah oil field and thereby, allegedly, stealing Iraqi oil. Feeling itself the aggrieved party, Iraq demanded a long-term commitment by Kuwait not to exceed its OPEC quota and further demanded that Kuwait and Saudi Arabia provide Iraq considerable economic aid. Kuwait initially acceded to the first demand (later, however, only for a three-month production limit), and Kuwait and Saudi Arabia agreed to provide Iraq with aid.

Given the decline of the Soviet Union, the Iraqis assumed that the United States would not see an occupation of Kuwait as a Soviet bid to control the Persian

Gulf. Further, the Iraqi leader had made it clear to the Americans that Iraq would guarantee, at a reasonable price, a continued supply of oil from the gulf. American military intervention seemed unlikely—certainly not as long as the other Arab states accepted the fait accompli of an occupation—and it was believed that an invasion of Kuwait would solve Iraq's two main problems: the urgent need for cash and the desire to control Būbiyān and Warbah. It also had the promise of giving Iraq the hegemony in the Persian Gulf that it desired.

It was under these circumstances that on Aug. 2, 1990, Iraqi forces invaded Kuwait. On the same day, the UN Security Council passed Resolution 660, condemning the invasion and demanding Iraq's unconditional withdrawal. It also called on Iraq and Kuwait to begin immediate negotiations. On August 6 the Security Council passed Resolution 661, imposing economic sanctions against Iraq that consisted of a wide-ranging trade embargo.

Ṣaddām showed no sign that he was prepared to withdraw from Kuwait, and on August 8 Iraq declared Kuwait to be its 19th province. U.S. Pres. George Bush and various allies, considering Iraq's action an act of blatant aggression as well as a threat to Western interests, decided that the status quo ante had to be reestablished, and U.S. troops began arriving in Saudi Arabia the next day. A 28-member coalition, including several Middle Eastern countries and led by the United States, mobilized sufficient military and political support to enforce the Security Council's sanctions, including the use of force. The coalition demanded that Iraq withdraw from Kuwait by no later than Jan. 15, 1991, but the Iraqis seemed unconvinced that coalition forces would actually attack and felt assured that, in the event of an attack, the large and well-equipped Iraqi military would hold up against U.S. and coalition forces long enough to inflict heavy combat casualties and sap American political resolve.

The coalition began air operations on January 17 and on February 24 commenced a full-scale ground offensive on all fronts. The Iraqi military crumbled rapidly and capitulated after less than one week of fighting on the ground. The defeat compelled Iraq to withdraw from Kuwait and accept the Security Council resolutions.

The military operations not only destroyed much of the Iraqi armed forces but also severely damaged the infrastructure of the major Iraqi cities and towns. The defeat encouraged the Shīʿite and Kurdish populations to rebel against the regime. In its action against the Shīʿites, the government forces killed many people and caused extensive damage. The attempt by Iraqi forces to reconquer Kurdistan forced more than a million Kurds to flee to Turkey and Iran. Many died from hunger and disease. Only with Western intervention did the Kurdish refugees feel they could return to their homes in northern Iraq. In April 1991 the United States, the United Kingdom, and France established a "safe haven" in Iraqi Kurdistan, in which Iraqi forces were barred from operating. Within a short time the Kurds had established autonomous rule, and two main Kurdish factions—the KDP in the north and the Patriotic Union of Kurdistan (PUK) in the south—contended with one another for control. This competition encouraged the Baʿthist regime to attempt to direct affairs in the Kurdish Autonomous Region by various means, including military force. The Iraqi military launched a successful attack against the Kurdish city of Arbīl in 1996 and engaged in a consistent policy of ethnic cleansing in areas directly under its control—particularly in and around the oil-rich city of Karkūk—that were inhabited predominantly by Kurds and other minorities.

Iraq's Shīʿite population fared even worse than the Kurds. Pressure on Shīʿite leaders to support the Baʿthist regime had begun even before the Iran-Iraq War, and although their failure at that time to endorse Ṣaddām's regime led to frequent attacks on Shīʿites and their institutions—Shīʿite leaders were killed and imprisoned, madrasahs were closed, and public religious ceremonies were banned—most Shīʿites had served faithfully in the armed forces against Iran and shouldered an inordinate amount of the fighting. Only after the Persian Gulf War did the Shīʿites rise up against the regime, and their rebellion was put down with great brutality. The U.S.-led coalition did not establish a safe haven for the Shīʿites in southern Iraq, and the regime subsequently put immense resources into excavating several large canals to drain the country's southern marshes, which had been the traditional stronghold of the Shīʿites. The regime allegedly killed scores of prominent Shīʿite religious and political leaders and arrested and imprisoned thousands of others whom they accused of sedition.

Within those regions of Iraq still controlled by the regime, Ṣaddām's control of society was strengthened by his continued domination of the country's internal security services, which had grown steadily since the 1970s and, under his close direction, had become a ubiquitous part of life in Iraq. Although the Shīʿites and Kurds suffered the regime's greatest wrath, enemies, or perceived enemies, of the Iraqi leader were consistently rooted out even among the Sunni Arab elite—including members of Ṣaddām's own family. All were dealt with brutally. The Iraqi leader survived several coup attempts in the 1990s, some of which were launched by disaffected members of the Sunni community, but the effectiveness of the security apparatus was proved time and again by its ability to preempt most attacks before they occurred and unfailingly to keep Ṣaddām in power.

The UN Embargo and Oil-for-Food Program

The UN-imposed economic embargo on Iraq remained in force during the Persian Gulf War but expired after Iraq withdrew from Kuwait. Since Iraq had refused to withdraw voluntarily, however, in April 1991 the Security Council adopted Resolution 687, which made lifting the embargo conditional on Iraq's accepting the demarcation of the Iraq-Kuwait border according to their bilateral agreement of October 1963, surrendering all its WMD, including missiles with ranges greater than 90 miles (150 km), and destroying the ability to create such weapons. The resolution also called for the establishment of a monitoring system, to guarantee Iraq's compliance.

The Security Council established a UN Special Commission (UNSCOM) to inspect and verify that Iraq was complying with the ban on WMD. By mid-1991, however, it was becoming clear that the embargo would very likely last longer than had been originally expected and that, in the meantime, the people of Iraq needed humanitarian aid. Thus, the Security Council passed a pair of resolutions establishing what came to be called the oil-for-food program, in which Iraq, under UN supervision, could sell a set amount of oil in order to purchase food, medicine, and other necessities.

The government of Iraq, however, rejected this offer on the grounds that it violated Iraq's national sovereignty. In addition, between 1991 and 1993 Iraq continually obstructed UNSCOM's search for WMD. The United States and the United Kingdom (and originally France) responded by carrying out intermittent air attacks on Iraqi military and internal security targets. Gradually, however, the Iraqi regime managed to render UNSCOM's work almost ineffectual. In the end the Iraqis argued that all of their proscribed weapons had been destroyed, although UNSCOM insisted that the Iraqi regime was still concealing a small stockpile of prohibited items and technology. In spite of ongoing Iraqi recalcitrance, the Security Council adopted new measures, which Iraq accepted only under the threat of economic collapse in 1996. In December Iraq resumed oil exports, and the first food and medicine shipments arrived in Iraq in March 1997.

In February 1998 the Security Council again raised the ceiling of the permitted sales of Iraqi oil, but Iraq continued to obstruct the work of UNSCOM, and there were fears that the country had resumed its programs for WMD, in spite of UNSCOM's verification and inspection efforts. In December 1998 the United States and the United Kingdom attacked military and government targets within Iraq—primarily those suspected of being associated with WMD—in the most intense bombardment since the 1991 war.

Following the raids, however, Iraq refused to allow UNSCOM personnel to reenter the country. Iraqi leaders also rejected a new, more liberal, resolution put forward in late 1999 and instead demanded that sanctions be lifted completely. By then, however, the embargo's effectiveness had begun to diminish. The easing of sanctions alone had allowed a greater degree of prosperity, and Iraq smuggled an increasing volume of material, particularly oil, to generate income, bring in proscribed items, and fuel consumer demands. This was facilitated by the fact that a number of countries, particularly those adjoining Iraq, derived great financial benefit from trade with that country.

In light of the deteriorating embargo—and always observant of the humanitarian toll that it produced—a number of states within the UN called for its complete abolition. Others sought to streamline the embargo by introducing what were termed "smart sanctions" that would be directed at prohibiting access to a much smaller, more specific list of materials to Iraq, including weapons and military technology. Iraq, however, refused such a program and again was able to have modifications to the existing sanctions sidelined within the UN, but it was unable to have sanctions lifted completely.

The Iraq War

Debate rapidly shifted, however, following a series of deadly terrorist attacks on the United States on Sept. 11, 2001. No clear connection was made linking Iraq with the attacks, but U.S. Pres. George W. Bush argued that the attacks demonstrated the vulnerability of the United States and that this vulnerability, combined with Iraq's antipathy for the United States, its desire to obtain or manufacture WMD, and its record of supporting terrorist groups, made the complete disarming of Iraq a renewed priority. At the insistence of the United States, the UN Security Council issued Resolution 1441 on Nov. 8, 2002, demanding that Iraq readmit inspectors and comply with all previous resolutions. After some initial wrangling, Iraq agreed to readmit inspectors, who began arriving in Iraq within two weeks.

The international community soon differed on the degree of Iraq's cooperation. Initial inspections were inconclusive, though a small block of countries led by the United States and the United Kingdom argued that Iraq had resorted to its earlier practices, that it was willfully hindering inspection efforts, and that, given the large volume of material unaccounted for from previous inspections, it doubtless continued to conceal large quantities of proscribed weapons. Other countries, particularly France, Germany, and Russia, sought to extend inspections and give the Iraqis further time to comply. The United States and the United Kingdom, however, were convinced that Iraq never intended full cooperation and began to mass troops and war matériel around Iraq in preparation for a military conflict.

On March 17, 2003, the United States and its allies declared an end to negotiations, and on March 20 they launched the first in a series of precision air attacks on targets in Iraq, followed by an invasion of American and British ground forces from Kuwait in the south. As U.S. troops drove northward, they met resistance that was sometimes heavy but was generally poorly organized. On April 9 resistance in Baghdad collapsed, and U.S. soldiers took control of the city. On that same day, British forces secured Al-Baṣrah, and Iraq's other major cities fell within days, sparking a short but intense period of rampant looting of stores and government buildings. Major fighting ended by late April, but acts of common criminality continued, and, as the months passed, a pattern of concerted guerrilla warfare began to unfold. On Dec. 13, 2003, Ṣaddām surrendered to U.S. troops when he was found hiding near Tikrīt, and major figures from the regime were tracked down and arrested.

Following the fall of the Baʿth Party, an entity known as the Coalition Provisional Authority (CPA), which was headed by a senior American diplomat, assumed the governance of Iraq. An Iraqi governing council appointed by the CPA had limited powers. The primary goal of the CPA was to maintain security and rebuild Iraq's badly damaged and deteriorated infrastructure, but its efforts were widely hampered by an escalating insurgency involving a variety of groups comprising both Iraqis and non-Iraqi fighters from other Arab and Islamic countries. Prominent among them were remnants of the former Ba'thist regime as well as a group under the control of Abū Muṣ'ab al-Zarqāwī, a Jordanian-born militant linked to al-Qaeda, the terrorist organization behind the September 11 attacks.

Responsible for countless killings and sabotage, the insurgents targeted coalition forces, new Iraqi security forces and recruitment centres, electrical installations, oil pipelines, and other civilian institutions. The resistance was concentrated mainly in Baghdad and the Sunni-dominated areas north and west of the capital, especially in Al-Fallūjah. A push by U.S. and central government forces failed to gain control of that city in April 2004, but a renewed effort succeeded in November. Major confrontations between coalition and government forces and those loyal to Muqtadā al-Ṣadr, a radical Shī'ite cleric, also occurred south of Baghdad, mainly in Al-Najaf and Karbalā'.

Meanwhile, efforts to hand over control of the government to the Iraqis continued. In June 2004 the CPA and the governing council were dissolved, and political authority passed to an interim government headed by Ghāzī al-Yāwar. Subsequently Ayād 'Allāwī was selected prime minister. U.S. and coalition forces remained. Although no WMD were unearthed, the discovery of mass graves and records found in the offices of Ba'thist intelligence services bore witness to the human toll of the atrocities committed by Ṣaddām's regime. Ironically, revelations of assault and mistreatment of Iraqi prisoners by U.S. soldiers at the Abu Ghraib prison near Baghdad brought their own international outcry. On Jan. 30, 2005, in spite of the ongoing violence, general elections were successfully held for Iraq's new 275-member Transitional National Assembly. Iraqis around the world were allowed to vote in absentia. In April 2005 Kurdish leader Jalāl Ṭālabānī was elected president of Iraq.

A draft constitution approved by a national referendum in October 2005 called for a new legislature, the

In the midst of violence, Iraq held a successful general election on Jan. 30, 2005. Wathiq Khuzaie/Getty Images

members of which largely would be elected from constituent districts (some members would be appointed). Sunni Arabs voted overwhelmingly against the new constitution, fearing that it would make them a perpetual minority. In a general election on December 15, the Shīʿite United Iraqi Alliance (UIA) gained the most seats but not enough to call a government. After four months of political wrangling, Nūrī al-Mālikī of the Shīʿite party Islamic Daʿwah formed a coalition government that included both Arabs and Kurds. Ṭālabānī, who was reelected as president in April 2006, nominated al-Mālikī as head of the new government, which was sworn in on May 20, 2006.

Political violence continued to grow. Attacks directed at coalition forces, which had begun to rise in 2005, became even more violent and sophisticated. Yet it was attacks against Iraqi civilians, mostly in and around Baghdad, that consumed the attention of the international community as Shīʿite and Sunni militia and terror groups targeted members of the opposite group. Many of these attacks were directed at the police and their families. Even with U.S. assistance, the Iraqi government had a difficult time recruiting and training police officers and soldiers to assume domestic security duties. The death of al-Zarqāwī in June 2006 did nothing to reduce the violence.

Ṣaddām was executed by an Iraqi court on Dec. 30, 2006. Shortly thereafter, President Bush proposed a controversial plan to temporarily increase U.S. troop levels by more than 20,000 to help stem the flow of violence—an effort that became known as the surge. By that time, Iraqis had grown increasingly weary of the violence, and American support for the war, which had come to be called simply the Iraq War, reached an all-time low.

Levels of violence in Iraq began to decline during 2007, and some of the additional troops deployed by the

Nūrī al-Mālikī

(b. July 1, 1950, near Al-Ḥillah, Iraq)

Nūrī al-Mālikī became prime minister of Iraq in 2006. Mālikī's grandfather was a prominent poet and briefly (1926) a government minister. Mālikī earned a B.A. (1973) in Islamic studies at Uṣūl al-Dīn College in Baghdad and an M.A. (1992) in Arabic literature at Ṣalāḥ al-Dīn University in Arbīl. In 1963 he joined the Da'wah, an underground Shī'ite political party. In spite of party splits, Mālikī remained faithful to the original faction. In 1979, facing persecution from Ṣaddām Ḥussein's regime, he left Iraq for Jordan and then moved to Syria and later Iran, where he arrived in 1982. The Iraqi government condemned him to death in absentia in 1980. In Iran he joined hundreds of thousands of Iraqi Shī'ites who had fled their homeland or been deported to Iran by Ṣaddām. Mālikī spent most of the decade of the Iran-Iraq War (1980–88) in Iran, and in 1989 he relocated to Damascus, where he became the head of the Da'wah Party's Syrian branch.

After U.S.-led forces toppled the Ba'th regime in April 2003, Mālikī returned to Iraq. He became deputy head of the committee responsible for purging former Ba'th Party officials from government jobs and was elected to the Transitional National Assembly in 2005. He served as the senior Shī'ite member of the assembly's committee that was charged with drafting the new Iraqi permanent constitution. In the general election of Dec. 15, 2005, Mālikī was reelected a member of the assembly as part of the United Iraqi Alliance (UIA), the Shī'ite bloc. The UIA won a plurality of seats and chose a Shī'ite, Ibrāhīm al-Ja'farī, another Da'wah Party leader, to be the first full-term prime minister. Ja'farī's candidacy, however, was opposed by the Arab Sunnis and the Kurds, who regarded him as a divisive figure. Following a four-month ministerial crisis, the UIA nominated Mālikī in April 2006, and he became the new prime minister. He formed a government of national unity with a cabinet that included not only UIA leaders but also members of the Arab Sunni, Kurdish, and secular blocs. Though known throughout his years in exile as Jawad, Mālikī decided in April 2006 to resume using his birth name of Nūrī.

Mālikī's prime ministership was marred by instability. Violent and intractable warfare between Sunni and Shī'ite militias and a rampant anti-American and antigovernment insurgency together created economic paralysis and a lack of security in the country. An increase in U.S. troop levels in early 2007 had some initial success in stemming the violence, but Mālikī failed to achieve any significant political progress. In March 2008 in Baghdad he met with Iranian Pres. Mahmoud Ahmadinejad, whose country supported Mālikī's government. This was the first visit by an Iranian leader to Iraq in nearly 30 years. Later that month Mālikī launched a government operation against the Shīʿite militia of Muqtadā al-Ṣadr in Al-Baṣrah, and the fighting ended only after Ṣadr ordered a cease-fire. Although Mālikī called the offensive a success, many believed that his government had been further weakened.

United States were withdrawn. The declining levels of violence were attributed not only to the surge itself but to a confluence of factors, including the Sunni Awakening—a movement in which Sunni tribesmen who had formerly fought against U.S. troops eventually realigned themselves to help counter other insurgents, particularly those affiliated with al-Qaeda—as well as a voluntary cease-fire observed by Ṣadr and his forces.

In November 2008 an agreement that determined a timetable for the final withdrawal of U.S. forces, which had been under negotiation for nearly a year, was approved by the Iraqi parliament. Under that agreement, U.S. troops were scheduled to leave the cities and towns by mid-2009, and withdrawal from the country was set to be completed in early 2012. In February 2009 newly elected U.S. President Barack Obama announced that U.S. combat forces would be withdrawn from Iraq by the end of August 2010, with the remaining troops due to pull out by December 2011. On June 30, 2009, after turning security responsibilities over to Iraqi forces, U.S. troops completed their withdrawal from the country's cities and towns as scheduled.

CONCLUSION

Iraq has long been a centre of great strategic importance. During ancient times the extensive alluvial plains of Mesopotamia (modern Iraq) gave rise to some of the world's earliest civilizations, including those of Sumer and Babylon. The region's fertility (which makes up most of what is known as the Fertile Crescent) supported not only civilization but also wealth, and it was later a valuable portion of various larger polities, including Persian, Greek, and Roman dynasties.

Following the rise of Islam in the 7th century, Baghdad was founded as the capital of the 'Abbāsid caliphate. In the centuries that followed, Baghdad became the most significant cultural centre of Arab and Islamic civilization, a world-renowned hub of arts and learning. Strife among the 'Abbāsids and attendant decline was capped in the 13th century by the arrival of the Mongols, who overturned the 'Abbāsids and sacked Baghdad. The assault put an end, for a time, to that city's ascendancy and set Iraq on a centuries-long path of decline.

Important land, education, and military reforms accompanied the emergence of Iraq as a modern nation-state. At the same time, the interest of European powers, in particular the British, served to underscore Iraq's value in an age of colonialist competition. With petroleum reserves among the world's largest, Iraq's strategic value was reemphasized in an entirely new way. British involvement was short-lived, and, following a turbulent monarchical period and subsequent instability, revolution brought Iraq under the government of the Ba'th Party, of which the most infamous leader was Ṣaddām Ḥussein.

With the support of its massive oil wealth, Iraq was able to pursue developments that included one of the

Arab world's largest armies, enabling Ṣaddām to pursue ill-fated conflicts with Iraq's neighbours, including Iran (the Iran-Iraq War, 1980–88) and Kuwait (the Persian Gulf War, 1990–91). In the Persian Gulf War the Iraqi invasion of Kuwait was met with the active opposition of the United States and a coalition of its allies. A decade later, the Iraq War (ostensibly fought over weapons of mass destruction) toppled Ṣaddām, ending Baʿth rule in Iraq. U.S. involvement in Iraq continued with the Iraq War (2003–), which exerted great influence over Iraqi society—and U.S. society, for that matter—as it continued through the first decade of the 21st century.

GLOSSARY

'Abbāsid dynasty A dynasty of caliphs (750-1258) that ruled the Islamic empire from its capital at Baghdad and claimed descent from 'Abbas, the uncle of Muhammad.

afforestation Establishing a forest, particularly previously unforested land.

alluvial Relating to land with sand, gravel, or clay deposited by flowing water.

armistice A temporary suspension of wartime hostilities by agreement of both parties; truce.

autonomous Not controlled by outside forces; independent.

caliph ("successor") A successor of Muhammad as temporal and spiritual head of Islam.

caliphate The office or dominion of a caliph.

calligraphy A decorative form of handwriting, in many societies considered the supreme visual art.

coalition A provisional alliance of diverse parties, persons, or states for cooperative action.

embargo A government order that prevents certain or all trade with a foreign country.

exile A state of compulsory absence from one's motherland.

fait accompli An accomplished fact; something already done.

garrison A military post.

gross domestic product (GDP) Total market value of the goods and services produced by residents of a country during a specific period of time, excluding the value of net income earned abroad.

guerrilla A person who engages in irregular warfare, especially as a member of an independent unit carrying out harassment and sabotage.

heretical Against the teaching of official religious doctrine.

hinterland An area located inland from a coast, or far away from a city or metropolis.

mawālī (singular: mawlā) In Islamic history, non-Arab converts to Islam.

Monophysite One holding the doctrine that Christ had a single inseparable nature that is at once divine and human rather than having two distinct but unified natures.

Nestorian Member of a Christian sect originating in Asia Minor and Syria holding that Christ had separate divine and human natures.

passion play A dramatic representation of the sufferings and death of an outstanding religious or spiritual figure.

pastoralist One whose life is based on the raising and herding of livestock.

personality cult A construct centred on the practice of glorifying a leader.

petrochemical Strictly, any of a large class of chemicals (as distinct from fuels) derived from petroleum and natural gas.

regent A person who governs a kingdom in the minority, absence, or disability of the sovereign.

war matériel Ammunition, weapons, and other military equipment.

weapon of mass destruction (WMD) Weapon with the capacity to inflict death and destruction indiscriminately and on a massive scale.

BIBLIOGRAPHY

Geography

Comprehensive overviews of Iraq may be found in Helen Chapin Metz (ed.), *Iraq: A Country Study*, 4th ed. (1990); Christine Moss Helms, *Iraq: Eastern Flank of the Arab World* (1984); Phebe Marr, *Modern History of Iraq*, 2nd ed. (2002), which includes a brief treatment of the land, people, and civilizations of the past; and Stephen Hemsley Longrigg and Frank Stoakes, *Iraq* (1958). Also useful are the yearly updated essays on Iraq in *The Middle East and North Africa* (annual); and *Middle East Record* (annual); and entries in *The Encyclopaedia of Islam*, new ed. (1960–2002); and *Encyclopedia of the Modern Middle East*, 4 vol. (1996).

The geography and social makeup of Iraq is explored in Gavin Young, *Iraq: Land of Two Rivers* (1980), which provides an excellent guide to the chief towns, the landscape, and the people; Edmund Ghareeb, *The Kurdish Question in Iraq* (1981), which explores relations with the Kurds; and Chibli Mallat, *The Renewal of Islamic Law: Muhammad Baqer as-Sadr, Najaf and the Shi'i International* (1993), which charts Ayatollah Ṣadr's influence on the Shīʿite religious thought in the second half of the 20th century.

Society, economy, and foreign policy are discussed by a number of Iraqi and Western specialists in Tim Niblock (ed.), *Iraq: The Contemporary State* (1982). Political development is discussed in John F. Devlin, *The Baʿth Party: A History from Its Origins to 1966* (1976), which details the growth of the Arab nationalist party of Iraq and Syria. A critical analysis of Iraq before the First Persian Gulf War is included in Kanan Makiya, *Republic of Fear: The Politics of Modern Iraq*, updated edition, with new introduction

(1998), originally published under the pseudonym Samir al-Khalil (1989). Amatzia Baram, *Culture, History and Ideology in the Formation of Ba'thist Iraq 1968–1989* (1991), deals with the regime's shifting national priorities and its changing views of nationalism. Ofra Bengio, *Saddam's Word: Political Discourse in Iraq* (1998), studies the official Ba'thist power language.

History

A general history of the Middle East in the early Islamic period may be found in Hugh Kennedy, *The Prophet and the Age of the Caliphates* (1986). A masterly discussion of the geography, religion, and society of late Sāsānian and early Islamic Iraq may be found in Michael G. Morony, *Iraq After the Muslim Conquest* (1984). Fred McGraw Donner, *The Early Islamic Conquests* (1981), examines 6th- and 7th-century Iraq and Syria.

Works on the 'Abbāsid caliphate and Būyid rule include Hugh Kennedy, *The Early Abbasid Caliphate: A Political History* (1981) and Roy P. Mottahedeh, *Loyalty and Leadership in an Early Islamic Society*, rev. ed. (2001). Studies of cultural life in the 10th century include Joel L. Kraemer, *Humanism in the Renaissance of Islam: The Cultural Revival During the Buyid Age*, 2nd rev. ed. (1992). On dynasties and ruling groups, the most useful reference is Clifford Edmund Bosworth, *The Islamic Dynasties: A Chronological and Genealogical Handbook*, enlarged and updated ed. (1996). John E. Woods, *The Aqquyunlu: Clan, Confederation, Empire*, rev. and expanded ed. (1999), is a useful treatment of the Turkmen period.

For viewing Iraq within the Ottoman context, the best general study of Ottoman history and institutions is Halil Inalcik, *The Ottoman Empire: The Classical Age,*

1300–1600, trans. from Turkish (1973, reissued 2000). The last decades of Mamlūk rule are the subject of Tom Nieuwenhuis, *Politics and Society in Early Modern Iraq: Mamlūk Pashas, Tribal Shayks, and Local Rule Between 1802 and 1831* (1982). Roderic H. Davison, *Reform in the Ottoman Empire, 1856–1876* (1963, reissued 1973), gives an excellent account of 19th-century Ottoman reforms, including information on Midhat Paşa's role in their implementation in Iraq. Meir Litvak, *Shi'i Scholars of 19th Century Iraq: 'Ulama' of Najaf and Karbala* (1998), is the best historical account of the Iraqi Shīʿites, charting developments within the Shīʿite religious establishment and its relations with the Ottoman authorities.

A good discussion of the British mandate period may be found in Peter Sluglett, *Britain in Iraq, 1914–1932* (1976), which is based on British documents. Reeva S. Simon, *Iraq Between the Two World Wars* (1986), gives an account of the development of pan-Arab ideology. Michael Eppel, *The Palestine Conflict in the History of Modern Iraq: The Dynamics of Involvement, 1928–48* (1994), discusses the interrelations between Iraqi domestic affairs and the Palestine question.

The Iran-Iraq war is discussed in pre-armistice works such as Shahram Chubin and Charles Tripp, *Iran and Iraq at War* (1988) and Edgar O'Ballance, *The Gulf War* (1988), which includes a detailed chronology and maps. Post-armistice publications include Hanns W. Maull and Otto Pick (eds.), *The Gulf War: Regional and International Dimensions* (1989). Both the Iran-Iraq War and the First Persian Gulf War are described well by Anthony Cordesman and Abraham Wagner, *The Lessons of Modern War*, vol. 2 (1991).

INDEX

C

D

E

F

G

H

I

J

K

L

M

N

O

P

Q

R

S

T

U

W

Z